DRAWN
FROM MEMORY

Ernest Shepard, 'Kipper' to his friends, was born in 1879. He attended art school at the Royal Academy and served in the First World War, after which he made his living as an artist and political cartoonist for *Punch* magazine. He was the definitive illustrator of numerous works including *Winnie the Pooh, Now We are Six* and other works by A A Milne; *The Wind in the Willows* and other works by Kenneth Grahame; and Richard Jeffries' *Bevis*. He died in 1976.

Green velveteen and a lace collar
at the age of seven

ERNEST H. SHEPARD

Drawn from Memory

METHUEN

Published by Methuen 2000

1 3 5 7 9 10 8 6 4 2

First published in Great Britain in 1957 by Methuen & Co Ltd
This paperback edition published by Methuen Publishing Ltd
215 Vauxhall Bridge Rd, London SW1V 1EJ

Copyright © 1957 E. H. Shepard

Methuen Publishing Limited Reg. No. 3543167

A CIP catalogue record for this book
is available from the British Library

ISBN 0 413 75300 X

Printed and bound in Great Britain by
Creative Print and Design (Wales), Ebbw Vale

Papers used by Methuen Publishing are natural,
recyclable products made from wood grown in sustainable forests.
The manufacturing processes conform to environmental
regulations of the country of origin.

TO
MY WIFE NORAH
AND
TO THE MEMORY
OF
MY SON GRAHAM

CONTENTS

PREFACE

THIS story tells of the period of my childhood when I was seven to eight years old. I was born in St John's Wood, at No. 55 Springfield Road, and I can remember the nursery there and the garden at the back. Each morning my father would come in and dance me round before he went to business. I can also remember the cotton frocks that I wore with plaid bows on my shoulders and a plaid sash round my middle; under these I wore little drawers, rather tight and scratchy for small legs. Getting ready for a party, Mother would frizz my hair with a curling iron.

We moved to No. 10 Kent Terrace when I was about four years old, and it was there that I spent the happiest days of my early boyhood, with Mother and Father, my sister Ethel and my brother Cyril. I was the youngest of the family and we were all devoted to Mother. She had a sweet and gentle nature and her beauty was enhanced by the colour of her hair—the colour of ripe corn, as I heard it described by an admirer.

It was soon after this story ends that she was taken ill. We children did not realize the seriousness of her illness and enjoyed pushing her wheeled chair on our walks round the Park. Her early death cut short our happy family life. We tried to put a brave face on it for Father's sake, and I remember telling my brother that I would not cry any more because Mother would not have liked it. It was years before the cloud seemed to lift and the natural buoyancy and happiness of youth revive itself in me.

When my own children were growing up I told them the story as I tell it here, recalling the incidents, one by one, as they came back to my mind. They would ask to have more about the Aunts, or the Farm, or perhaps Martha and Lizzie. I think that their first visit to a pantomime must have been just as exciting as mine was, but, when I described my pantomime feelings, my son asked that I should one day 'write it all down and make a story of it'.

The drawings of the people and places are as I remember them. Both No. 10 Kent Terrace and No. 53 Gordon Square look today very much the same from the outside as they did seventy years ago. Standing on the Terrace, as I was a few days back, I almost expected to see Lizzie's face appear at the area steps, telling me to bring in Septimus and wash my hands for dinner. I was once again just a little London boy.

E. H. S.
February 1957

Chapter One

SEPTIMUS

A COLD wind was blowing down Park Road as we three children, with Martha our nursemaid, passed St John's Wood Church and, crossing over, came in sight of the flagstaff on the roof of the public house on the opposite side of the road. A flag had been hoisted, a light blue flag, and it meant that Cambridge had won the Boat Race. Ever since I could remember, both my

'It was a light-blue flag'

brother Cyril and I had looked forward eagerly to the race, though we had never seen it. We were staunch Oxonians; the only reason for this was that our favourite uncle Willie, the clergyman and St Paul's master, who was father's eldest brother, had been at Balliol College. My sister Ethel, on the other hand, was for Cambridge; she would give no reason for her preference, and we boys always suspected it was because she thought light blue the prettier colour. In any case, there it was: Cambridge had won this year; there was no doubt of it.

Sunk in gloom, I trailed along behind the others, and as they passed the spot where road crosses canal, I stopped and hauled myself up on the wooden paling. I knew that by peering over the top, I could see the canal, dark and sinister, below. It was just possible I might see a corpse floating on the water, such as the old messenger man at the corner of the Terrace had seen. But even that consolation was denied me, and in obedience to a call from Martha I turned and trotted after the others. I was still brooding over this when I caught up with my brother and sister, and Cyril was able to remind me that there would be another race next year, which Oxford might win. Much comforted by this thought, I dismissed the subject from my mind before we reached our home at No. 10 Kent Terrace.

The house is still there. It stands in the middle of the row and is ornamented with stucco columns in front and a small balcony to each drawing-room window.

The Terrace lies back from the main road and has a garden in front. There used to be railings all round, but these have now been replaced by a wire fence. The railings were unclimbable by small boys, and too close together for them to squeeze through. There was a lock on the gate, for which we had a key but it was very stiff to turn. The garden was untidy, with some big trees and a lot of sooty shrubs, but it was an excellent place to play in because no one ever disturbed us there.

I was rather proud of the front door of our house, for it was distinguished by having two stained-glass panels which my father had designed. One was called 'Night' and the other 'Morning'. 'Night' had an owl in it, which enabled me to tell it from 'Morning'. Behind the front door there was a little hole where the key of the garden was kept.

'With the hapless doll attached'

The front dining-room was separated by folding doors from the smaller back part, which we used as a playroom. Over the fireplace in the front room was an overmantel of wood, with shelves, also designed by Father, and filled with a collection of blue and white Nankin china, a type of ornamental pottery then in vogue.

The hall was paved with tiles and the staircase was of stone with iron banisters. It was wide, and open enough for us to play our favourite game of parachute descents. This pastime had been a craze with Cyril and me ever since we had been taken to the Crystal Palace and had seen a certain Professor Baldwin make the perilous descent from the main transept. Lit up by limelights and accompanied by the din of a brass band and the thunder of drums, he had sailed

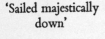

'Sailed majestically down'

majestically down, to arrive in the arena in tights and spangles, and to bow his thanks to a delighted audience. When we came home we set about emulating him, but wisely decided to try the experiment first with Ethel's dolls. Ethel was older than we were and her interest in dolls was waning, so she took the conscription of her dolls in good part. This was fortunate, for the casualty rate was high. Woe betide the wretched victim if her head was made of china or wax! We soon found that an umbrella was of little use as a parachute; it became unmanageable and stuck. Then we tried handkerchiefs of various types and sizes, one of which was decorated with a coloured picture of the Professor himself; but even these proved unsatisfactory. Poised at the top of the stairs, leaning over the banisters and holding the contraption with the hapless doll attached, I would launch it while Cyril waited below, prepared to avert calamity. The only doll to survive was Minna, grubby, tough, and made of leather.

The Terrace was paved with flagstones, and had gas lamp-posts with $\boxed{\begin{array}{c} \text{IV} \\ \text{G.R.} \end{array}}$ on the base, which Martha told us meant a king. There were round iron coal-hole covers at regular intervals, and these would make a loud clank, clank when ridden over by Septimus.

Septimus was my pride and joy. He had arrived, carefully packed, on the tenth of December, my seventh birthday, and been christened Septimus by my father. The horse was a gift from my Godmother-Aunt. Cyril and I always thought there must have been some direct divine influence working on my behalf to guide Aunt Alicia on this occasion, leading her away from the more useful gifts; and that the Angel Gabriel, disguised as the shopwalker in Mr James Shoolbred's store, had led her to Septimus where he stood, with eyes dilated and distended nostrils, pawing the air with his two forelegs as though yearning to discard his three wooden wheels. It was some days before

16

I mastered him, but after that I would carry him down the front steps and pedal along the Terrace, 'clank, clank', to the end and back again, my little legs spinning round till Septimus and I stopped for lack of breath, or the face of Lizzie, the cook, appeared at the area steps to say that dinner was ready. Tethered to a lamp-post, Septimus would then await his master's pleasure.

There was generally someone with whom to pass the time of day

'The Angel Gabriel, disguised as the shopwalker'

on the Terrace. If it wasn't one of the tradesmen's boys it was Ellen the milk-woman. Ellen had been my nurse before Martha came, when Cyril and I were of very tender age. She had been with us until she married, and used to push us in the double perambulator. We sat side by side and squabbled most of the time. The pram was like a wide chair on three wooden wheels, the smaller wheel being in front. It had a canopy hood which folded up like an umbrella made of green material with a fringe which I enjoyed picking off. There was an apron to cover our legs, with a strap across our middles. It furnished a very bumpy ride, especially when crossing roads, which were badly metalled in those days. Almost the first thing that I can remember is trailing round the Park and being lifted from the pram to feed the ducks by the ornamental water.

'Tethered to a lamp-post'

Sometimes we would go as far as the Zoo and look through the bushes so that we could see some of the animals in their cages and hear their various noises or the raucous shriekings of the parrots. Then we would pass the Botanical Gardens and come to the Enclosure, a slice of the Park reserved for the residents who lived in the houses opposite. The Enclosure had oak railings along the road side which were sufficiently widely spaced to allow anyone as small as myself to squeeze through. It had been a game with Cyril and me, until he grew too big, to sneak through and, avoiding the eye of the Park Keeper, run along inside. Dodging from bush to bush, one could go quite a distance. If spotted, one broke cover and made for the railings. The Keeper, in his top hat and with a stick under his arm,

'Trailing round the Park'

was too dignified to run after us and would content himself with shouting.

Ellen was a sturdy woman and made light of the long walks. When she left to get married, she took a job at the dairy. Carrying the cans of milk, she came round the Terrace in the morning and afternoon. She had two cans, slung on a wooden yoke across her shoulders and over her plaid shawl. She would put down the cans, and tip some milk into the waiting jugs from a tin measure, any that was spilt being quickly lapped up by our black Sambo and the other

19

cats who always followed her. If Martha or Lizzie were there she
stayed for a gossip. Her husband was named Jack. According to
Martha, he never would work and sometimes beat Ellen. He was an
ill-conditioned, lanky fellow, who was to be seen, more often than
not, leaning against the palings by the Windsor Castle.

'All the cats would follow her'

Once a week the dustmen came round. They had a grey horse
which seemed permanently to wear a nosebag, and which moved
slowly along the Terrace, pulling the open four-wheeled cart. The
horse would stop every now and then while the men, who wore

leather flaps at the back of their hats, clattered up and down the area steps and emptied their baskets into the cart. Martha and Lizzie always went round shutting doors and windows against the flying dust, and if I were out on the Terrace on Septimus, I had strict orders to bolt indoors quickly. The same thing applied when the coalman came. I would watch him from the dining-room window as he tipped the coal sacks into the hole with a distant sound of rumbling from below. Then one day I thought I'd like to see what happened when the coal came down, so I sneaked downstairs, slipped past the kitchen and dived into the cellar. I could hear the coalman above heaving the sacks about, then down came an avalanche of coal and I was nearly choked. Covered with coal dust, I found the door and staggered out, to find myself face to face with Lizzie. She told me I ought to be ashamed of myself, and led me upstairs, where I was undressed, scrubbed, and threatened with direst penalties should I ever do it again.

'Reminded me of a respectable stork'

At the top of the Terrace was a high wall, behind which were the grounds of Hanover House. There are large blocks of flats there now, where once were pleasant gardens. It was by the high wall that there sat, day in and day out, the old messenger man. He sat on a box with his back against the wall so that he commanded a view of the whole

Terrace. Beside him in a canvas bag was his lunch. He appeared to spend his time sleeping, but he would spring to life if any householder

'Had once given him a penny'

appeared at a front door to wave or call to him. His mission in life was to do odd jobs or to 'run' errands, though he had never been known to break out of a walk. He was tall and lean and wore a threadbare grey tail coat which was too small for him. He always reminded me of a respectable stork. In a spasm of generosity I once gave him a penny, which the old man pocketed after dubiously spitting on it. He always knew where to find a cab when one was wanted and repeated whistling had failed to produce it.

'The butcher's boy'

I suppose the most popular caller, anyhow among the cats, was the cat's-meat man. He came twice a week with his hand cart, which was decorated with painted boards on each side reading, 'Purveyor of choice meat for cats and dogs.' The meat was cut in slices and stuck on a skewer. It cost about threepence.

The butcher's boy was the pick of the tradesmen. He came round the Terrace in a smart little pony cart with a very well-groomed pony, brown with white stockings, and harness as clean and bright as new pins. The boy sat perched up on his driving seat, wearing his striped blue apron and with his hair plastered down with mutton fat. The pony trotted very fast and would pull up sharply. The boy would then run round to the back and shoulder his meat on a wooden carrier. He was down the area steps and up again in a jiffy, the pony starting before he was fairly back on the box. None of the other tradesmen was half so smart. The baker had only a hand cart with a basket hanging at the back.

Then there was, of course, our own particular policeman. He often came round in the dusk of an evening. Slow of movement he was, but wise, and given to good advice.

Park Road, with its wide pavements, was almost countrified then, and we got to know all the shops. First after the Windsor Castle was Chaplin's the fishmonger. Then came Kensit the greengrocer, with Mrs Kensit stout and motherly in her bonnet. Further along was Mr White the chemist, with large coloured glass bottles in his window and a strong smell of medicine as you passed the shop. Beyond that was the upholsterer and cabinet maker, Mr Grahame, who had a broad Scots accent. Maltby, the tailor, had an important-looking coat of arms over his shop, and at the end, built into the wall, close to Clarence Gate, was the little dressmaker's shop with its two round-topped windows and door between. Then, just at the top of Upper Baker Street, was what Martha called the Victoria Wining Shop, where a friend of hers served behind the counter. At the upper end of Park Road, on the opposite side, where is now a big garage and block of flats, by the top of Upper Gloucester Place, stood Coles the linen draper. Quite an important shop it was, with windows full of the latest fashion in hats and a fine display of long lace curtains. Mother was never allowed to leave the shop without having her attention drawn to 'Our latest line, fresh from Nottingham.'

Nearly all our shop assistants in those days were young men, even in the drapers' and the chemist's.

Behind Coles' shop, where are now the marshalling yards of British Railways and the approach to Marylebone Station, was an acreage of small and pleasant Georgian houses, as there are to this day around Lord's Cricket Ground. They had brick-walled gardens and quiet roads. It was there, in a tiny white house in Boscobel Place, that father and mother lived after they were married. Mother often told us how happy they were there, and what heart searchings the faithful Lizzie suffered before leaving grandma to come to them.

We passed all the shops as we three children, in charge of Martha, went to school in Upper Baker Street. Ethel went to the Church of England High School for Girls, and we boys to the Kindergarten attached.

The Kindergarten was down a yard, where now stands British Railways Lost Property Office. The yard was paved with concrete and served as a playground. We had invented a sort of football adapted to this ground. Played with a rubber ball, it included certain hazards such as drain pipes, and there were penalities for going outside into Baker Street. At the lower end of the yard was a high brick wall, but, by climbing on a stack of timber, we could look down on Baker Street Underground Station and see the trains steaming in and out. It made our clothes dirty, and Miss Parkman would come out when she saw us there and clap her hands and in we would have to go.

There were three mistresses, Miss Parkman, Miss Turner and Miss Gardner. I liked Miss Turner best. We had morning prayers up in the big schoolroom, and Canon Holland came once a week to talk to us. There was a boxed-in staircase leading to this classroom, and the door at the top was firmly shut when prayers had begun. When we were late we had to wait, in silent shame, in the dark, to emerge and be admonished after prayers were over. On the whole Cyril and I liked going to school; the work was not too hard, and there was plenty of time for play; also we had made several friends, and there were some grand toys in the cupboards for wet days. 'The Fighting Cocks', real feathered birds operated by wires, were a special treat and only allowed out under strict supervision. Then we were encouraged to make gifts for our parents; paper cards would be decorated with coloured wools after being pricked in patterns; drawing was encouraged, but coloured chalks were not popular as they always made a mess.

'The fighting birds'

The school house, which was on three floors, had been a workshop. All the kindergarten children gathered in the big downstairs room for morning break. There was eager competition for the post of 'Bun-buyer' which, ever since the disaster to the bag of hot buns that had burst in the middle of the street, had fallen to the lot of one of the eldest. After the pennies had been collected, the bun-buyer would go to the baker's across the road and come back with a bag full of steaming hot buns. It was the fashion among the boys to flatten their buns by pressing them, sometimes under foot, to gain an effect of size.

The classroom where I was taught was on the top floor, and was presided over by Miss Gardner. There were benches and long desks, but we were not trusted with ink-wells and always used pencils or slates. There was a big stove, which one tried to get near in cold weather. Among the pupils were Nigel Playfair and his sister Audrey. Then there was Willie Rayner, whose father was a doctor in Dorset Square. Cyril and I often went with Willie and some of our other

'Duly flattened'

friends to play cricket in Paddington Recreation Ground. We had a bat and a ball but had to use our jackets for a wicket, until one day a friend of Willie's turned up and brought some stumps. His name was George, a tall youth in white flannel trousers, whose father, George Grossmith, was acting in *The Mikado*. George said he wanted to be an actor too.

Among all the girls it was Helen Clowes whom I liked best. Helen had something wrong with her spine and had to lie on a board all the time. We boys would try to get the end seat so as to be near her, to hand her books or pencils. She had dark curly hair and grey eyes and was very quiet. She would say 'Thank you' in a gentle voice for the small services she was rendered. She was only at school a short time, and one day Miss Parkman called us together and told us that Helen had died.

Afternoon school ended early, and sometimes Mother came and fetched us. This was a special treat, as it meant that we might get a bus ride to Oxford Circus and help her to do some shopping. Cyril and I found the women's shops very dull, but these expeditions generally ended by our going to Elphinstone's, the teashop in Regent Street, where we could get cream and other delicious cakes, or better still, ices.

It was getting on for Easter when a large parcel arrived at No. 10 Kent Terrace. From the fact that this was hastily put away out of sight by Mother, Cyril and I suspected it might possibly be a present for us. Mother's great friend Gussie had been known to give liberally before now, and a large Easter egg might contain anything, even a steam engine with rails for it to run upon—things I had always longed for. After I had gone up to bed, I lay in my combinations and pondered, while Martha was airing my nightshirt over the gas-jet. She passed the garment backwards and forwards over the globe, casting strange shadows on the ceiling like clouds in the sky. I questioned her closely. 'Martha, have you seen it? What shape is it? Is it heavy, and does it rattle?' But it was no use. Martha, intent upon her airing, would give me no answer beyond 'Now, Master Ernest, don't you go asking me a lot of questions. You know what curiosity did to the cat.' As a matter of fact I didn't, but I had to give in. Tucked up in bed I thought of every possibility, and when Cyril came up too I tried to get an opinion from him. But he had brought up his stamp album and was too much excited over a stamp that his

'Where you could get cream cakes'

Ethel + Cyril with E + Mum

uncle, Mother's brother, had sent him from Natal to bother with Easter Egg speculations.

When I woke on Easter morning it was some time before I remembered, then I hopped out of bed. It seemed a long business

'Airing my nightshirt over the gas'

washing and dressing, and it was not till after breakfast that we had our presents, and the parcel was produced and opened on the dining-room floor.

It *was* a great big egg, gaily coloured and decorated with a gold frill round the join in the middle. Inside was a red box with a black and gold label: 'Pontoon Train. Made in Germany.' Wrapped up in paper were soldiers in blue uniforms with spiked helments, little

horses with harness that would take off, and little carts filled with
tiny wooden planks and surmounted by boats. It was all very exciting.

Dear Gussie had given us a 'train', but it was the wrong kind.
Nevertheless, Cyril and I spent many happy hours with the blue
soldiers. We built a bridge with the wooden planks and the boats;
then our whole army, horse, foot, artillery, black savages and all,
marched solemnly across. It was at dinner time that Mother brought

'Pontoon Train. Made in Germany'

up the awful question of 'Thank-you' letters. She said we must get
down to it and write ours before we forgot. This was a horrible
task which Cyril and I both hated and always put off as long as
possible. It was all right if Ethel was there. She was older and full of
brilliant ideas. She would have the thing done in no time, and it
would only remain to be copied out, but that afternoon she had gone
along to the Lloyds' to practise the Toy Symphony. So Cyril and I
settled down in gloomy silence to make the best of it. I had made
several false starts when I decided that I needed inspiration, and what
better way of achieving that than a ride on Septimus? So I fetched him
from his stable at the back of the house, carried him down the front
steps, and proceeded to rattle up and down the Terrace.

What with the fresh air and the excitement of the ride I forgot
all about my letter and was only recalled to earth when Mother

appeared at the front door and called a halt. She asked if I had written my letter. I could only answer that I had done some of it. She looked worried and asked: 'How much?'

'Well, not very much.'

'We'd better go in and see,' she said.

So I tied Septimus to his lamp-post and in we went. Cyril was deep in his stamp album, and by the look of satisfaction on his face I guessed that *his* troubles were over. Mother bent over the table and picked up the ink-stained results of my labours. With furrowed brow she read out: 'Dear Gussie I hope you are quite well . . .' She looked at me sternly for a moment, and then burst out laughing. 'It's not very much, is it?' she said. Then: 'Perhaps we had better do it together.'

This we did, and it was the grandest 'Thank-you' letter I had ever written. When it was finished, addressed and stamped, I was able to remount Septimus and ride him, in triumph, to the pillar-box at the corner and post both our letters. It required a certain amount of horsemanship to keep Septimus under control while doing this, for he was apt to shoot away from underneath when I was reaching up to the slot, but by turning the front wheel sideways he could be kept quiet. Then I waited at the corner, as I always liked doing, to watch the traffic go by.

There were not many buses, but in the hot weather their horses would be given a drink at the trough in front of the Windsor Castle. I could see this from the end of the Terrace. One day a man riding a high bicycle fell off, right over the handlebars. Mr Chaplin, the fish-monger, ran out and helped him up and then sat him on a chair and mopped his head with a rather fishy sponge.

Once a week all three of us had a music lesson. We had violins of different sizes and were taught by Mr Cruft. He had a long beard and talked about Herr Joachim. His son is now teaching the violin to young people.

It was dreadfully tedious having to play scales and my fingers never seemed to be in the right places, but it was better when I was promoted to Boccherini's *Minuet*. By that time Ethel could rattle along with *The Caliph of Baghdad*. We boys were not to be allowed

'My little fingers never seemed to be in the right place'

to play our fiddles in the coming Toy Symphony, and it was only after the most urgent appeals that Cyril was given the warbler thing, filled with water, that he blew into, while I got the triangle.

Soon after Easter, after the Miss Dicksees had been to tea, Mother told us that there were plans for Father and herself to go abroad, and that Polly, Minnie, and Frank Dicksee might join them in a trip to France. This was all very well for them, but oh how I hated it when Mother was away! I had been known to express myself very forcibly on the subject. On one occasion, at a tender age, I lay on my back in the middle of the high road in Ripley and kicked and yelled till the whole village was roused.

3   33

'Kicked and yelled in Ripley'

Cyril and I were filled with suspicion about this new trip and brooded darkly upon what was to be our fate while our parents were away.

Chapter Two

THE AUNTS

THE Aunts lived in the corner house in Gordon Square, a very big house with a portico in Gordon Place. It had been built by my grandfather, an austere gentleman who was quite bald and always wore a wig. He felt the cold and generally wore, in addition to his overcoat, a plaid shawl wrapped round his shoulders. This, in combination with the wig, caused much amusement among the younger elements at Lloyd's of which he was a member. The Aunts told how they watched the new house being built from their back windows in Tavistock Square, and how Grandfather kept an eagle eye on the proceedings. The old man died soon after it was finished, and his widow lived there with her grown-up daughters till she too died. I remember her, in her stiff black silk dress, with a white cap

'He felt the cold'

and side ringlets, giving me spoonfuls of crystallized coffee sugar. But that was before our story begins.

There were four aunts. The eldest, Aunt Alicia, was my Godmother. Aunt Annie was an invalid who spent the day lying on a couch, which it was difficult not to bump against; she had a nurse who kept a canary, called George, in a cage outside her window. Then there was Aunt Fanny, the smallest but by far the most energetic; and finally Aunt Emily, stout and short of breath. There were a lot of maids, and Mrs Lamb, the charwoman, and Henry, the odd man who cleaned the knives and boots and didn't seem to be quite right in the head, or, as Aunt Emily more delicately expressed it, 'was a little touched'.

'Giving me spoonfuls of crystallized coffee sugar'

It was the Aunts who suggested that we three children should stay with them in the Easter holidays while our parents went abroad with the Dicksees. Though stoutly opposed by Cyril and myself, the visit was arranged, and promises were wrung from us to behave well and make the best of it.

We said 'good-bye' to Martha and Lizzie and Black Sambo with gloomy hearts. I came near to open revolt when I was told that to

aunt Fanny

'By far the most energetic'

aunt Emily

'Stout and short of breath'

aunt Alicia

'My godmother who always felt the cold'

take Septimus was out of the question. We and our bags were finally stowed in a four-wheeler.

Things began to look brighter when we arrived at Gordon Square and found that the morning-room had been set aside for our use and we were to have tea there, with buttered scones, by ourselves. Then,

'A stone urn for visitors' cards'

the front door of the house had narrow windows on either side through which one could peep at visitors outside. In the hall was a hard and forbidding chair for the use of the less respectable callers. There was also an elaborate mahogany hat-stand with two men's hats (Father's cast-offs) to strike fear into the hearts of such burglars or other Lawless Men as might effect entry by the front door. On one side stood a great sideboard with a marble top, supporting a stone urn for visitors' cards. On the wall above was an albatross's head with mothy plumage and faded glass eye. Someone must at one time have had an urge to brighten the scene, for on the wall hung an incongruous framed picture from a Christmas number showing a little girl sitting up in bed giving pink biscuits to a dog. The stairs, which led up and up, had ornamented iron banisters. The dining-room was painted a dull green and was rather dark, with large bookcases; an enormous mahogany sideboard took up almost one end of the room, and on the walls were: (1) a mezzotint of the Duke of Wellington, (2) an engraving by Landseer with a lot of game lying about and a man who looked like the Prince Consort, and (3) several Martin engravings of Biblical scenes. All the furniture

'More proper to have a hip bath in your own bedroom'

was of solid mahogany, and not very comfortable, and there was always a slight smell of dinner.

Cyril and I found that we had separate rooms, which was a nuisance as we couldn't talk after going to bed. Taking a bath was going to be difficult too, for although a bathroom existed at the very top of the house, the water in it was never hot and it was rarely used. Ladies considered it much more delicate and proper to have a hip bath in their own bedroom.

The Aunts dined at six o'clock, and we children were given High Tea at the same time. The only drawback to this feast was that all

'A string of maids'

hands had to be clean, faces washed, and shoes changed. Afterwards there was generally a round game of cards in the drawing-room. Aunt Alicia had a horror of fire, so the only lamp allowed was one which burnt a sort of oil that had to be pumped up; but as the thing gave no light anyway, that didn't matter. There were also six candles on the table. At a quarter to nine tea was brought in. Though Cyril and I were generally already as tight as drums, we would find room for more, particularly for a specially choice brand of biscuit. Blown out and sleepy, I then went to bed. It was something of a shock when my godmother came up with me and made me say my prayers out loud. Of course I got muddled, and kept repeating my-self. Finally I was told I would be given a little book suitable for a boy of my age, which gave all the prayers from A to Z. Oh dear! I had to learn several. They kept me awake at night, and I never, never got them quite right.

Down in the drawing-room at ten o'clock proper prayers were said. A string of maids filed in, led by Mrs. Edlin the cook, followed

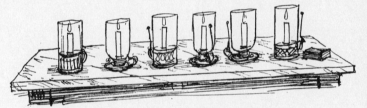

'Time they were carried up to bed'

by Jane the parlour-maid, then Alice and Mary, and the little one at the tail. There was always a whispering outside, and a suspicion that eyes were peering through the crack of the door to make sure that Aunt Alicia had found her place in the book and was ready. On the marble slab in the hall was an array of polished brass candlesticks with glass shields and metal extinguishers. They were lit as a sign that it was time they were carried to bed.

The large Square in front of the house had a promising look, but it was disappointing when, after taking the key that hung on the hat-stand, we crossed the road and opened the gate. There was a large stretch of grass, but this had a notice 'Keep Off'. Moreover there was a man with a broom and a barrow to see that you did keep off. Then the grimy laurel bushes and shrubs led to dirty hands and clothes, which meant retaliation from the household. To climb trees was forbidden. Altogether it was a poor substitute for Kent Terrace, and we boys preferred to stay and play in the morning-room.

'Sweep the dust into two neat borders'

Near the gate at the corner of the Square a crossing sweeper had his pitch. I felt sorry for him, for his eyes were always watering, and sometimes he looked very cold. If the weather was wet and the road muddy, he swept clean a path across, and if it were fine and the road dusty, he would sweep the dust into two neat borders with a curl at each end. He wore an old bowler hat, and had a special—and newer—one on the pavement for pennies.

There were certain days when the Aunts used to shop. Aunt Fanny was the active one, and did most of this. She would take Ethel with her. Cyril and I did our best to keep out, but were trapped and conscripted more than once. First there was the dairy in Torrington Place, where large china urns with polished brass lids stood on the counter, and where we could have a penny glass of milk dipped out for us. Next door was John's, the stationers, with this week's *Punch* open in the window. Then Shoolbred's, in Tottenham Court Road. Apparently there was a

'The keeper with the goldbanded hat'

rivalry between this shop and Maples', and I could not get it clear why the Aunts would not go to Maples'. Aunt Emily, whose explanations never gave satisfaction, said it was something to do with a four-in-hand, and that it was 'raffish'. This called forth an expostulation from Aunt Alicia. 'Emily! where did you learn that horrid expression?'

Aunt Emily's attempts to ward off searching questions as to why

'Spend the afternoon in the drawing-room'

there were gates with a lodge attached at the corner of Woburn Square were met with little sympathy, and she had to fall back on saying it was to keep out rough people. But the keeper with the goldbanded hat didn't look equal to keeping out rough people, any more than did the beadle at Marylebone Church, or the inspector of nuisances.

On Sunday we went to St Pancras Church. It was the only occasion that I saw my godmother go out, for, like her father before her, she felt the cold, and was swathed in shawls and cloaks. When we got back to Gordon Square, Cyril and I were horrified to find our playroom had been tidied up, the few toys and games we had brought with us put away in a cupboard, and the order had gone forth that we must spend the afternoon in the drawing-room. No old *Punch* or *Illustrated London News* volumes to look at: instead, *The Sunday Magazine*, *Leisure Hour*, and *Sunday at Home*. The Aunts rested or knitted garments for the

'I followed the pattern most carefully'

people of Algoma. Aunt Emily had her own special activity, which was in aid of the Deep Sea Fishermen. The garments she knitted, which were of fearful and wonderful proportions, were often tried on Father, who was inclined to make derogatory remarks, while Emily, with puzzled looks, and a knitting-needle in her mouth, would say, 'Tut-t-t, very odd, I know I followed the pattern most carefully,' and, 'But then, Harry, you must remember they are very *big* men.'

As the afternoon wore on, the only cheerful sound was the ringing of the muffin man's bell as he came round the Square. But, alas! he was allowed to pass unheeded.

Mr Paget was the Rector of St Pancras, and the curates used to make duty calls on the Aunts. It is recorded that, on one occasion, while they were returning the call of a newcomer, and were waiting in the sitting-room, the Aunts saw on the mantelpiece a TOBACCO PIPE! And that was the end of that call.

But there were happier days when Aunt Fanny took us to the Tower of London, and I got all worked up and involved in long discussions on armour and culverins with the Beefeater, and we saw the Golden Crowns and the places where people were tortured. . . . All most enthralling.

Then there was the party at Dr Davis's. Dr Davis lived opposite. It was a real children's party, with lots of good things to eat, as well as ices, but there were some grown-ups, including a man with a loud booming voice who kept us in roars of laughter. His name was Whymper, and Mrs Davis told us he used to climb mountains.

There was no piano at Gordon Square, which was hard lines on Ethel, who was learning that instrument and was getting on very well. Normally she practised most diligently. We had not brought our violins with us as our parents were afraid the scraping would worry the Aunts. So I was surprised when my godmother asked me one day if I would like to go to a concert and hear a great violinist play. Aunt Alicia knew that I learned the fiddle; indeed I had played my 'piece' to her on more than one occasion, though I do not think she was much impressed. She had kindly thought of the concert as a special treat for her godson. I accepted the invitation with alacrity and was told that Sarasate was giving a recital at the St James Hall and that my aunt would get tickets. The concert was in the afternoon,

'On the mantelpiece a TOBACCO PIPE!'

and I went with Aunt Fanny. I had never been in a concert hall before and was rather disappointed with its general appearance. I had expected a stage and scenery, a gaily decorated curtain and lime-lights, and here there was just a platform with a very large piano. There were banks of flowers on either side, but that was all.

However, I ceased to worry about this when the great man began to play. I know that I was deeply moved. It was a revelation to listen to the music that he got from his fiddle, and to watch his delicate white hands fingering so perfectly. I could not explain what I felt when I tried to thank my godmother afterwards. I never, never dreamt that such music was possible, and I felt quite hopeless about my own efforts.

Sitting in the drawing-room after tea, our Aunts would tell us of their childhood. Aunt Alicia, being one of the eldest, remembered more than the others. She told us how the family had lived on two top floors of the big house in Tavistock Square. With no form of heating, the rooms were icy cold in winter. Hot-water bottles were unknown, and, except for an occasional bed-warmer for delicate little Mary or Annie, they had to freeze. The marvel is that they survived at all. At certain times the children were taken downstairs to see their parents, which meant endless cleaning, tidying, and dress-ing up in little starched underclothes and low-necked muslin frocks with short sleeves. Most of their lives were spent in a large, cheerless playroom, which was never warm enough. Then the daily walk was purgatory. No running wild in the Square, but a prim little procession of underclad children with blue noses, chapped wrists and ankles, who were glad to get indoors again. In the summer they were just as uncomfortable, though not so cold, for the holland dresses that they wore were hard and scratchy.

There were eleven children, seven girls and four boys. Aunt

Mary, the eldest, died before I was born, as did Richard (a very dapper-looking Uncle, to judge by the family album), about whom the Aunts were inclined to be sentimental. It was suggested that his early death was due to a disappointment in love. There were many sighs, and he was generally referred to as 'Poor Richard'.

My godmother, Alicia, came next, then Willie, our favourite Uncle. Aunt Ellen, the fourth, had left the maternal home some years before, to go off and live on her own in Bournemouth. Tended by a Scots maid called Ganson, who came from the Shetland Isles, she lived to a great age.

Then came Annie, the invalid; Robert, my godfather, whom we rarely saw; Fanny, who possessed as much energy as all the others put together; my father, the youngest son; and Emily the youngest child of all, always rather short of breath.

Before Gordon Square was built, my grandfather had built a house in Guildford, on Guildown. There the whole family went for their summer holiday, year after year. Richard Shepard, his brother and my great-uncle, had also built a house on Guildown Road, so that the two families were much together at that time. There are photos, again in the family album, of croquet parties on the lawn of Guildown House, including one of my great-aunt, a woman of character who could never be persuaded to face the camera. It shows her standing in bonnet, shawl, and crinoline: back view.

We children were glad when, at the end of twelve days, we heard that our parents were back. Eagerly we packed our things and went out in the Square in the morning. As Cyril and I came back into the house for midday dinner we sensed an air of gloom. Indeed Aunt Alicia was lying down in her room, and Aunt Emily was distinctly snappish. We had a dreadful feeling we might be to blame and I tried to think over my conduct of the last few days. We kept out of

4

the way in the playroom till Father came. He greeted us, and then went upstairs.

He was gone some time, so I crept up to the landing to listen, and came back to report that they were all talking very seriously. I had

'Sitting on the dustman's knee'

heard Aunt Alicia say: 'Do you think we should send for William?' Presently Father came down and, carefully closing the playroom door, burst into laughter. Then he revealed the awful truth.

Only that morning Aunt Alicia had descended into the kitchen and found the cook sitting on the dustman's knee.

Chapter Three

SCARLATINA

My parent's friendship with the Dicksees was of long standing, for Mother had known them as a child, and their father Thomas Dicksee had painted a portrait of Grandma. Frank was an Associate of the Royal Academy and was considered to be one of the rising artists. He had a studio on Campden Hill, at the top of Peel Street. My brother and I, dressed as choir boys, were his models in a big picture he was painting. The studio was up a rather narrow flight of stairs. His housekeeper, a kindly woman, made us feel at home during the sittings.

Before Sending-in Day for the Royal Academy my parents were invited to Show Sunday at Frank Dicksee's studio. They took, besides my sister, us boys, which was rather a rash thing to do. We were severely tidied up and packed into a four-wheeler. When we reached the studio we found a lot of people and carriages. There was not much room to pass on the stairs, but I was forging ahead when the door at the top opened and a lady came out followed by an old gentleman. He had white hair, a white beard, and a florid face, and obviously I was in his way. My mother clutched my shoulder and drew me back to allow the old man to come slowly down. As he passed he bent down and gave me a smile. Mother, in rather a breathless voice, whispered, 'That was Robert Browning, the poet,' which, I fear, did nothing to impress me at the time. Up in the studio we were announced by a man in a brown coat and brass buttons.

'Collapsed with a mighty crash'

In the crush it was rather hot and stuffy and difficult to see the pictures, so Cyril and I found our way to the back, where we knew there were two suits of armour on stands. These we proceeded to investigate. Presently we undid certain straps. It was a most interesting business finding out how the various pieces fitted together, and it kept us amused for quite a time. Until, that is, I tried to climb up to reach the helmet. This was too much. The stand collapsed with a

'Mostly concerned with battle scenes'
Drawn by me in 1887

mighty crash and the assembled company turned round and stared at us lying among the debris. My poor mother, covered with shame, gathered us up and we were ignominiously taken home.

Some of my early efforts at drawing were shown, with a certain pride, by my father to his artist friends. Father had quite decided that I should be an artist when I grew up, though I myself considered an artist's life to be a dull one and looked for something more adventurous. There was a box full of these drawings which my father had saved. They came to light many years later, and showed that I was gifted with a somewhat lively imagination, mostly concerned with battle scenes.

It was on the first of May that I had one of the frights of my life. I was playing alone in the Terrace garden when I heard the jingling of bells and went to the end of the garden to investigate. A motley group of men rigged up for 'Jack-in-the-Green' was turning into the Terrace. One fellow, completely covered with greenery, so that only his legs were showing, was jigging up and down. Another had

'Jack-in-the-Green'

his face smeared with paint to represent a clown, and a third, in striped cloth coat and trousers, with a huge collar and a blackened face, was beating a tambourine. But the one that really frightened me was a man got up as a woman, in a coloured, ill-fitting dress, a wig made of tow, and showing brawny arms above dirty white gloves. Brandishing a tattered parasol, he, or she, held it out to catch coins thrown by passers-by or from the houses. Fascinated, I watched their progress from behind the bushes. Then I made a bolt for home. But I had left it too late. As I emerged from the gate the man-woman spotted me and came prancing up, calling out, 'What have you got for Jack-in-th'-Green, little gentleman?' Petrified with fear, I ran

'I was up in a jiffy'

back into the garden, and made for the sloping tree we always climbed. I was up it in a jiffy, but the dreadful creature, grinning like a satyr, followed me into the garden and started to dance around, while the others clattered and banged and shouted encouragement from the gateway. I was fast losing my reason when a welcome face appeared at the area steps—it was Lizzie. She took in the situation at a glance and up she came. Her indignation was more for the state of my clothes than anything else, but the enemy gave way before her and, blowing kisses and still dancing, the troupe passed on. I must have been almost hysterical when I was taken in and washed, and I never could bear the sight of a man dressed as a woman after that.

I do not know if I was in a weak state, but not long after that I was taken ill. It was by no means a serious illness, but enough to upset the routine of the household.

One Sunday evening I did not feel well. Cyril and I had been playing in the Terrace garden during the afternoon—our usual game of making swords out of iris leaves and having fights with them—and Father and Mother and Ethel had gone out to supper. As it was Martha's evening out we boys went down and sat in the kitchen. Lizzie was stitching in her armchair, and Cyril was nursing Sambo. I felt drowsier and drowsier; such a headache came on and I began to feel very hot. I told Lizzie that I did not want my supper. This made her look up. 'Why, Master Ernest, how flushed you look!' she exclaimed. When I said I wanted to go to bed, she realized something was genuinely wrong. I was packed off to bed in the back room upstairs and given lemonade to drink. There I felt hotter and hotter and thirstier and thirstier and oh, how my head did ache! When Martha returned she came upstairs and sat beside me. She put her hand on my head and tried to make me comfortable. The blind was not drawn and I could see the three ladies on the house in Hanover

'She grew larger and larger'

Terrace, beyond the mews; made of plaster, they stood on the cornice in classical attitudes. My favourite, the plump one, with the garment which only partially concealed her charms, seemed much in evidence, and, as I watched, she grew larger and larger and, detaching herself from the pedestal, began to float about in the air. Meanwhile all sorts of funny things were going on in the mews below. A tram clanged along, the top crowded with people shouting and letting off fireworks. It rushed up and down, as on a switchback, over the chimney-pots, then down to the yard and up again. Meanwhile the plaster lady floated nearer and nearer, till she drifted right into the room and stood by my bed. She seemed to be speaking. 'Why, Ernest darling!' But it was Mother's voice, and there was Mother home from her party. Now at last I could feel safe.

I was able to tell her about my head and feeling so hot. She sat down by me and put her cool hand on my forehead. After a while she went to the door and called: 'Harry, I think you had better ask Mr White to come in the morning.' I was feeling too sick to protest. This was the Mr White who had the chemist's shop in Park Road; he dispensed and doctored; and, though his cough mixtures were harmless and palatable, he had a dreadful concoction called 'White's Cleansing Powders'. They were taken in a spoonful of strawberry jam, but the jam always seemed to go down and the powder to remain stuck in the mouth. I had impressions of Mother coming in during the night in her dressing-gown and giving me lemonade. In the morning my head was not so bad, but my skin felt hot and itchy, and I didn't want to eat anything.

Mr White duly came, and a faint odour of chemist's shop came with him. He sat down by the bed and felt my pulse, looked at my tongue and examined my chest, and then said I'd got something called 'Scarlatina' and I must be kept away from Ethel and Cyril.

Sheets, saturated with carbolic, were to be hung on the landing out-side, and only Mother was to be allowed to see me, and then . . . out came the cleansing powders. It was some consolation to have a thing with such a long name.

It must have been a trying time for Mother, though it passed pleasantly enough for me. I fear I was a peevish patient. She was kind and gentle, as she always was, and would read to me by the

'Out came the cleansing powders'

hour. There was a serial called *Dolly and the Boys* which was full of all sorts of adventures going on and on, but it was a nuisance having to wait for the next instalment. I missed my brother and sister very much. It was not long, however, before I was allowed to talk to them over the banisters, provided they didn't come too close.

In bed, by myself, I lay and listened to the gurglings of the cistern in the loft, and to all the strange attendant noises that accompany any form of water circulation. I had plenty of time for rumination. When tired of drawing, I would lie back and consider some of the experiences of my short life. There was, for instance, the time that we stayed at Eastbourne. I could only just remember this, but I know that there was a balcony outside a large window on the first floor. Of an afternoon my mother and two of the Aunts who were staying

'Talk to them over the banisters'

with us would sit and do their needlework in the sunshine, while my sister, aged about seven, sat beside them on a stool. Every day about the same time there came along the sea front a man selling cockles and winkles. He was a strange figure. Pushing his handbarrow and calling his wares, he would sing, or rather recite, in a loud tuneless voice the lines that he made up as he went along. There was

something different for each house. Opposite our balcony he stopped and taking off his hat to the ladies, sang:

I see a flock of sheep,
In the midst a little lamb,
I wish my Mary Ann were here,
I wish my Mary Ann.

This chant became quite a household call with us but Aunt Emily would quote it on most inappropriate occasions.

I remembered very well my first introduction to sea-bathing. Father and Mother had been in for a dip and had taken Ethel with them. Cyril and I were handed over to

the tender mercies of the Bathing Woman. This formidable female was dressed in a serge bathing dress and a straw bonnet. She had red and brawny arms and her skin looked as if it were covered with

'I see a flock of sheep, In the midst a little lamb'

61

barnacles. As she spent most of her life in the water, this may even have been the case.

Her method was simple: the more difficult subjects, like my brother and myself, were tucked under her arms, where, our tender skins suffering acutely from contact with the rough serge, we were carried out to sea. The protesting body was then ducked, not once but several times, according to how the victim took it. The more he

yelled, the more the duckings, until, nearly asphyxiated, he was reduced to silence. The torturer, meanwhile, in what was supposed to be a soothing voice, repeated, 'Dippy go under, dear!' with each immersion, though her final remark to me did not sound like that. It took a lot to reduce me to silence and I was handed back to my parents with the comment: 'Well, that's the last I want to see of 'im!'

'Her method was simple'

One other thing that happened during our stay at Eastbourne caused a short-lived excitement. My father and a fisherman named Tyrrell, who often went fishing together, took a boat out for a day's sport. They had failed to notice the red flag hoisted on the Redoubt as a warning that the local Company of the Volunteer Artillery was to engage in some target practice. Sitting with their lines out, the fishermen were startled by the sounds of gunfire followed by the whizzing of projectiles over their heads or ricocheting on the sea to plunge finally below the surface. This lively activity went on for a time, the chief actors lying on the bottom boards of their boat, until someone must have noticed their situation and given the order to cease fire. My father and Tyrrell seized the opportunity to pull for home, to find on reaching the shore a crowd waiting. The rumour had gone round that the boat had been sunk. A rumour which, by good fortune, had not reached our lodgings.

It seemed a long time before I could go out, and when this was permitted Mr White said it must not be with the others; but I had at least the consolation of riding Septimus again. I was told not to scratch, but this was a difficult instruction to obey for my skin irritated and little scales would come off. Mr White said I would not be well until this stopped.

One day Father came and said that I was to go to the seaside for a week. This was grand news, and worth a lot of illness. It was better still when he said that mother and I could go all the way to Ramsgate by steamer. I nearly burst with joy when, our bags packed, we drove in a four-wheeler to the quay below London Bridge where the paddle steamer lay ready. She was crowded, for the trip was a special excursion to see the Fleet, which was lying, so the sailors said, at the mouth of the Thames. Everything was new and exciting, and I explored as much of the ship as I could, even clambering up on the paddle-boxes and having to be hauled back. There was a notice board by the man steering: 'Do not speak to the man at the wheel.' We went past Greenwich, and a man who seemed to know all about it pointed out the old fort at Tilbury. Great ships kept coming and going, and we saw strings of barges being towed along.

Many of the passengers had baskets of sandwiches, and there were lots of bottles of beer. When Mother and I got hungry, we went down below into a stuffy little saloon and had cold meat and pickles. The steward who served us said 'she was a steady boat', no doubt to reassure us, but as the sea was quite smooth nobody seemed to be sick. As the river widened out and the shores faded away in mist there was a general stir of excitement. Someone had seen masts ahead, and a sailor was pointing to where ships could dimly be seen. Everyone tried to crowd forward to get a first glimpse of the Fleet.

The sight, as we drew near, was an impressive one. The great ships were lying at anchor, guarding the mouth of the Thames. Square-rigged iron-clads, or flatiron turret ships, they lay, bristling

'Great ships lying at anchor'

with guns, with shining yellow funnels, white tops and black hulls. Our little paddle boat passed quite close to one great ship with *Northumberland* on her stern, and there were many knowledgeable men on board talking of the advantages of this or that, and saying 'Ah, yes, *Devastation*, no, *Thunderer*—must be *Inflexible*,' and no one to tell them whether they were right or wrong. I hung on to the rails at the stern, gazing, till the ships faded from view and I thought what a lot I should have to tell Cyril when I got home again.

It must have been late in the afternoon when we were put ashore at Ramsgate, and Mother and I, leaving our bags in charge of a porter, went in search of lodgings. There were many houses with

'Apartments' in the window. We chose one that looked promising but wasn't when we got inside; it smelt musty and the woman had a very red nose. So we tried another, which we liked better. The woman who answered the door was young and cheerful, though

'Took the dog and me out for walks'

talkative. She told us she had only been in the house six months. She promised to send down and get our bags from the porter when her brother came in. She had an old mother, and a little rough-haired dog, and her name was Miss Smyth. She proved to be kind and friendly and took the dog and me out for walks. Mother and I each had a bedroom, and there was a sitting-room with a balcony looking on the sea.

Down on the front we could walk along to the little harbour, and Miss Smyth, her dog and I would go along to the end, passing an old man who had a penny-a-look telescope on a stand. One day

'The sailors were very friendly'

Miss Smyth, who seemed to know everything that was going on, came in and told us there was a warship lying off the harbour. Greatly excited I was, and Mother took me down to the front and along to the telescope man, where I paid my penny and stood on a box and had a good look at the ship. The man said she was a torpedo-boat, and when I complained that she was very small, he said, 'So

is a wasp but it can sting all right.' He reckoned she would be there
several days, and I pestered Mother to let us go out in a boat, as
many people were doing, to see the ship close up. She promised
that, as Father was coming down in two days' time, we would do so
when he came.

I watched that ship in fear and trembling lest she should up
anchor and slip away, and when Father did come I gave him no
peace till we were safely packed in a rowing boat and launched. It
was disappointing to come up alongside such a small ship. By standing on the seat, held firmly by Mother, I could get my hands on the
rail and pull myself up so that my eyes were level with the deck.
The sailors were very friendly and one of them took the covers off a
Nordenfelt gun and showed us all the barrels, and then pulled a
torpedo out of its tube, shining like a great fish, but
I don't think I believed him when he said it would
blow up a big ship.

We had to go home the next day, but, before we
left, my father took me down to the shops to buy a
new hat, my sailor cap having fallen into the water in
the excitement of seeing the torpedo-boat and, after
being fished out with a boat-hook, was in rather poor
condition. It took us a long time to choose one. The
hats they showed us either did not fit or were all
wrong. At last we fixed on one, and though I did not
like it, it was not as bad as the rest. It was grey, with
a peak. I was doubtful about the peak, but Father said
it was all right. When we arrived home and showed
it to Mother, she was horrified. 'Harry!' she said,

'I was doubtful
about the peak'

'whatever induced you to buy a thing like that? Why, it's like . . .
someone in Struwwelpeter.' I hated it from that moment, and

would never wear it in London. I did, however, put it on to greet Ethel and Cyril just to hear what they would say.

When we reached home it was comforting to find everything tidied up, though there was still a smell of carbolic upstairs. It was nice to be able to run freely around the house again. Ethel and Cyril were out for a walk with Martha and I was allowed to go and meet them. I guessed they would come from the Park through Hanover Gate, so I mounted guard close to the Keeper's Lodge, and presently they hove in sight. I stood at the corner and waited. They were quite close to me before they recognized me, and when they did they just gaped at my hat, and we all laughed about it.

I was back at school again next day, rather proud of my ailment. It was something to have had an illness with such a big name. All the girls seemed to be talking about the new frocks they were to have for the coming Jubilee, and one of them boasted that her parents were going to take her to see the procession. The weather was growing warmer and we were able to go and play cricket in the afternoons with some of the other boys, either at Paddington Recreation Ground or else in Regent's Park. The draw-back to the latter was that there were often a lot of other games going on at the same time, and if we did not watch our ball closely it got stolen.

One day some tickets for the Zoo were sent to us, I think by a Fellow, as they were valid for Sunday mornings when the Zoo was closed to the general public. Mother took Cyril and me, and as the Keeper allowed us to go behind the barrier, we were able to see some of the animals quite close. There were no elephant rides going on, but I did not mind that; on the one previous occasion when I had been treated to a ride, I had had to sit on the elephant's head, and as I was wearing only a pair of thin flannel knickerbockers, the creature's sharp hairs came through and my poor behind was tender for days.

On that occasion, too, a small girl who was sitting on the double seat behind dropped her doll's hat. She shouted to the keeper below, who was walking in front of the elephant. 'Sorry, Miss,' he replied, 'it's gone inside.' She burst into tears.

There was a tunnel in the middle of the Zoo grounds that was a grand place for playing trains. It gave an echo as one ran backwards and forwards. The elephant went along it on the way to his house and looked far too big to get inside, but he just seemed to fit. As he passed by he picked up with his trunk any bits of biscuit or paper lying about— all 'went inside' like the doll's hat.

There was a bear-pit with a stout post in the middle, up which the bear would climb and sit at the top, with his mouth

'Sorry, Miss . . . it's gone inside'

open, waiting for buns to be thrown in. But it was always time to go home long before I had seen all that I wanted to see.

One morning at half-term my father had to visit the City to see my uncle about something, and he took me. On the way we stopped at Father's office in Great Marlborough Street, where he worked with another architect. I was glad to see the office. It had interesting plans and photographs of buildings hanging on the walls. A young man who was tracing things on a big board showed me a pair of compasses and explained how to use them. I was so fascinated by the instrument that my drawings for some time after that had as many circles as I could get in, all drawn with a small pair of compasses which Father found for me. We went on from the office by Underground to a station near the Bank of England.

My uncle was a member of Lloyd's, which was then housed in the Royal Exchange, and, as we walked through the city streets, I was amazed to see that every man seemed to be in a hurry. Also that there was hardly a woman to be seen in the throng. Lloyd's was upstairs and was filled with the same hurrying crowd. Father gave our names in the doorway and we found Uncle Robert sitting on a stool and throwing pellets of blotting paper about. He was rather deaf and had to bend down and put his hand to his ear when I tried to speak to him. When he and Father had done their talking it was time for dinner, and Father took me to a chop-house. The floor was covered with clean sawdust, and we sat at a wooden table in a little partitioned cubicle. I had a most delicious chop and felt rather grand and grown-up.

When we arrived home Ethel was having her piano lesson in the drawing-room. Her teacher was a friend of ours; we all called her Jessie, which was also Mother's name, though Mother was named Harriet as well. Ethel practised most diligently and would play her pieces to visitors without turning a hair. When the lesson was over, Jessie would often play for us, which we found a great treat. She lived in a small room in Mornington Crescent and I think she must have been very poor because she never seemed to go about at all and Mother often asked her to have a meal with us.

It was while we were having tea that the subject of an outing was raised. We children had been reading about Hampton Court Palace, and were anxious to see it. Mother then had the bright idea of us all making a day of it and taking Jessie with us. So it was arranged, and on Saturday morning we sallied forth. I remember that it was a wet day. I was very much impressed by all that we saw.

Hampton Court Palace

The grand red-brick building with its imposing gateway, wide staircases and spacious grounds seemed a fitting place for a king to live in. Once inside we went through gallery after gallery of pictures and one room full of weapons hung in patterns on the wall. The older pictures pleased me most and I studied these carefully. There was one of the Field of the Cloth of Gold, with a horse prancing just like Septimus. There was also an Elizabethan subject with a procession of knights and men-at-arms, and Queen Elizabeth herself

71

in an elaborately jewelled dress at their head. This absorbed my attention for a long time.

We had a midday meal at a shop on the green opposite the palace, and then walked across to Bushey Park to see the avenue of chestnut trees, all in full bloom. I would gladly have gone back for another look at the pictures but we had to think about getting home.

The first thing I did when we were back was to rush upstairs and get out my copybook and all the pencil ends that I could find. I drew pictures of Elizabethan processions, knights, horses, halberdiers, kings, queens and all. One drawing still survives. It was found in the box of my drawings which father collected and which lay for many years among the debris in the loft.

'One drawing still survives'
This was drawn after my visit to Hampton Court

Chapter Four

JUBILEE

Hooray! Hooray! for Jubilation Day!
'Tis only once in fifty years, so people say,
We all got mixed, and had a jolly spree,
A' going with the missus to the Jubilee!

CYRIL and I picked up this refrain from the local tradesboys, and we sang it about the house. The third line ran 'We all got *tight* and had a jolly spree', but Martha, with her strict sense of propriety, objected, insisting upon a more respectable word, so we reluctantly agreed to substitute 'mixed'. I do not think that Mother and Father would have raised the same objections, but the Aunts had to be considered.

It was early summer, and London was getting all dressed up for the great event. Along Park Road flags were sprouting, and V.R. signs with fairy lights were being fixed up. In the window of Coles the linen drapers, the usual display of long lace curtains had given place to rolls of brightly coloured material and a riot of flags of all nations. Small Union Jacks were on sale at $4\frac{1}{2}d$. each, complete with stick. Larger flags of many countries could be bought for $1s$. $1\frac{1}{2}d$. I had saved up two shillings and sevenpence, so I felt justified in investing in one of the larger kind. As Cyril and Ethel had each bought a Union Jack, I thought a change was called for. After due deliberation I chose one in red, yellow and black. I also bought, for $2\frac{1}{2}d$., a piece of bright red ribbon to make a bow for Septimus. The shopman could not help me in identifying the nationality of my flag, but when I got my purchase home Father told me it was Belgian and asked why I had chosen it. He went on to suggest that it should be displayed in a less conspicuous position than the others. Rather crestfallen, I

'Cyril and Ethel had each bought a Union Jack'

carried it upstairs. The window of our bedroom seemed a fitting place, and with a piece of string I tied it to the window ledge. Waving proudly in the wind, it made a brave show from the room, but the effect was disappointing when seen from the Terrace below, where it was quite outshone by the Union Jacks fluttering from the lower windows.

We heard wonderful tales of the decorations being put up in the main streets. Martha had been to see them, and we were delighted when Mother said she would take us to Oxford Street to see them for ourselves. We went after luncheon, boarding an 'Atlas' bus at the corner of the Terrace. Cyril and I were allowed to clamber up the steep steps, helped by the conductor, and were then handed along by the passengers, who sat back to back on the long middle seat. There was no railing to prevent one from falling off, only a low board, so we clung tightly as we were handed forward. I was first, and in consequence secured a place on the box seat beside the driver, where a man made room for me and fixed the tarpaulin apron.

'The effect was disappointing'

It was fun sitting beside the driver. The horses seemed to know of their own accord when to stop, though there were no regular stopping places, the bus halting where anyone might choose. The conductor stood on a little step at the back, by the door. He gave the signal to start by slapping the side of the bus with the strap by which he held on. Directly the horses heard the strap, and the driver released the foot brake, they strained forward and broke into a slow trot. The buses were painted different

75

colours, green, red, blue, or yellow according to the route, and had names like old stage-coaches. The 'Atlas' which ran up to the 'Eyre Arms' from the West End was light green, and the express 'City Atlas' was dark green. The 'City Atlas' ran in the mornings and could be watched from the breakfast-room windows bucketing past

'It was fun sitting beside the driver'

Kent Terrace, drawn by three horses at a fine gallop; the top was always filled with top-hatted men with fluttering newspapers.

A woman was never seen on top of a bus, the climb up was too steep for the long skirts worn at the time, though a young friend of Mother's called Poppy once clambered up to the consternation and horror of the inside passengers.

Inside a bus it was always rather hot and stuffy. The seats had a hard velveteen covering which stuck to the clothes, and in cold weather there was straw on the floor. The windows were adorned with coloured advertisements pasted on: 'Lamplough's Pyretic Saline', 'Rowland's Macassar Oil', 'Monkey Brand Soap'. Still, it

'To the consternation and horror of the inside passengers'

was fun riding on a bus; but if one *had* to travel inside, a four-wheeler was better, and a hansom—a very rare treat—best of all.

We enjoyed our ride to Oxford Circus. There seemed to be such a lot going on, such a bustle in the air. At Portman Square the bus turned along Wigmore Street because of the crush and eventually stopped near St George's Hall. Crowds of people were slowly

77

moving along; workmen were putting up boards in front of the shops; there was a babel of voices and hammering. As we pushed our way forward, Mother told us to be sure and keep close to her.

The Circus was gay with colour and bunting. Garlands of paper flowers were going up and a triumphal archway was being erected

across the top of Regent Street. Supported on striped poles it bore a large notice:

'VICTORIA!'

'ALL NATIONS SALUTE YOU!'

in gold lettering, while down the street other notices hung from house to house as far as the eye could see, saying: 'EMPIRE', 'JUBILEE', and 'BRITISH ISLES'.

Many of the shops had stands built in front of them, the wood-work being covered with yellow-fringed red baize. Men on ladders were fixing large wire crowns and V.R. signs on which fairy lights could be hung. On one or two of the larger shops were great stars, to be lit by gas, with 'GOD SAVE THE QUEEN' or 'LONG MAY SHE REIGN' underneath.

It was very hot and the crowd made it more so. Judging by their clothes, many of the people were up from the country. Hawkers were doing a roaring trade in favours and flags. Presently there was some excitement towards Regent Street and the crowd began to move apart. A body of soldiers marched up and stopped at the Circus. Now, I knew a lot about soldiers, and was able to inform Mother that they were not in full uniform. It was very exciting. The soldiers stopped and formed line in the middle of the street, while an officer paced out distances. The man selling flags said they were rehearsing to line the way on *the* day. It got hotter and hotter and we were very glad when Mother said we would get some tea at Elphinstone's.

We sat down at a marble-topped table and Mother ordered—(oh joy!)—ices. Glass plates with good big dollops and wafer biscuits were brought and soon eaten. Replete and happy, though very tired, we went home and were sent to bed early.

Jubilee Day dawned grey and misty, but the flyman who came to fetch Father and Mother very early, said it was going to be a hot day. The parents were going to join the Dicksees in seats to see the procession, while we were going with Martha to Regent's Park to see the Parade of the Boys' Brigade and of school children.

Mother came downstairs looking lovely in a new dress; it was striped blue and white with lace at the neck and sleeves. She wore a tiny bonnet, gay with flowers, and white gloves. She also carried a

'Looking lovely in a new dress'

very small parasol with a hook over her arm. I had never seen her look so beautiful. Father was very formal in frock coat and top hat, but he had a flower in his buttonhole. They drove off and we waved from the doorstep as they turned the corner of the Terrace.

At ten o'clock we children sallied forth with Martha. Lizzie, with Sambo adorned with a pink bow in her arms, gave us strict injunctions to mind the crowds and stick close to each other.

'The procession came in sight'

Out in Park Road people were already streaming through Hanover Gate, making for the Park. The Keeper at the Lodge had new gold braid on his hat and his buttons fairly shone. Martha was rather agitated and kept repeating her warnings to keep close to her, which was difficult. Along Hanover Terrace the crowd was very thick, so Martha asked a policeman to help us across to the other side. The policeman, who was a little stout and old, said he was a Reserve, as all the regular police were down in the West End.

The crowds began to be swollen with lots of children and these were gradually guided to where the procession was to come, so Cyril and I found ourselves in the front row. There was a lot of pushing and surging back and forth, but we managed to keep our places.

Presently the procession came in sight, led by the band of the Boys' Brigade. The drum-major, wearing a sort of busby with a plume, was a wonderful sight. He had gauntlet gloves and a sash across his chest and flourished a staff, throwing it around like a juggler. Some of the bandsmen were very young, but all were blowing away lustily and I was filled with envy of the drummers, the big drummer particularly, for he had a leopard-skin that nearly reached the ground. What fun it would be, I thought, to have a big drum and bang it along the Terrace!

When the procession had passed, the crowd began to break up, drifting into the Park to sit on the grass and refresh themselves. It was so hot that we were glad to get back home and have some cool lemonade and then lie down. Father had promised to take us out in the evening to see the illuminations.

Before I lay down, I went to the top drawer in the yellow chest and took out my copybook, the one I always drew special things in, and, with the pencil Mother had given me from a dance programme, I tried to draw some of the events of the day. Somehow, nothing would come right, the pencil would not work, suck it as I might.

I was nearly asleep when I heard the sound of horses. It wasn't just cabs or buses. It was something much more exciting. Tumbling out of bed I ran to the window in time to see Her Majesty's Royal Horse Artillery, busbies, shell jackets, yellow braid and all, with an officer resplendent in his blue and gold uniform riding in front. Behind him, on a white horse, rode a very young trumpeter. Then came the guns, rattling along. I had often seen the gunners exercising their horses, but never, never had I seen them in all their glory. I knew that they were on their way back to barracks in Ordnance Road, for sometimes our walks took us that way and then I would linger in front of the sentry, stiff and smart with his carbine on his arm.

Here was something worth drawing, but still the pencil would not work. I had given it up as a bad job when I heard the sound of my parents coming in. Mother came upstairs looking rather white. She said she had a headache, and was going to lie down, so I had to keep all my questions about the Queen and the Procession till another time. The house was very still after the excitements of the morning, but people could

'I would linger in front of the sentry'

be heard singing about the streets and there was a constant murmur of distant noise.

We were told to keep quiet because of Mother's headache, so after lying down as long as we could, Cyril and I crept down to our playroom. Presently I heard the organ man and went to the window

83

of the dining-room to look out. He was an Italian and had his organ
slung on his shoulder with a stick to support it. Sometimes he had a
monkey, but not today. He would come slowly along the Terrace
looking up at the windows, and if he saw us, would lean over the
railings, holding out his greasy hat and calling on all his saints to
bless us, which they would only
do if we gave him some money.
At intervals he would break into
song:

> *Viva la Français!*
> *Viva l'Italia!*
> *Viva Garibaldi!*
> *Victor Emmanuele!*

He sang this now with gusto
and a show of white teeth, but
it was hardly suitable for Jubilee
Day.

It seemed a long time after
tea before it got dark enough
and we were allowed to start
lighting our illuminations. The
fairy lights in coloured glass
shades had to be fitted with
night-lights and carried out to

'Viva Garibaldi'

put along the balcony outside the drawing-room. I insisted on lighting one of these, and made a mess of it, scorching my fingers and
dropping the taper inside the glass, where it sputtered. Then I had
no better luck with the Chinese lantern, which I have since found
is always difficult to light. This time I set fire to the paper, and the

whole thing went flaming into the area below. Further attempts were then stopped by Father. When all the illuminations had been lit, we trooped down and out of the front door to see the effect. It was not so good as the house three doors away, but still it was very gay.

Cyril and I were jumping up and down in our eagerness to get started, but first we had to sit down and eat some sandwiches and drink a glass of milk. Mother came downstairs, her headache better, and, to my joy, she said she would come with us; so off we all went.

There was a glow in the sky, and Park Road, usually rather gloomy after dark, with only a few gas lamps, was now a blaze of light. People were out in the street or else gossiping by their front doors. Coles the linen drapers had a beautiful star sign in flickering gas with V.R. at each side. Most of the houses had fairy lights along the window sills. The little dressmaker's shop near Clarence Gate had rows of candles in the windows and Maltby the tailor was particularly

'Flaming into the area below'

grand. But it was only when the bus landed us near Oxford Circus that the full glory burst upon us.

Almost every shop had some sign lighted up with lamps or gas, and a number of people in the crowd were carrying lighted Chinese lanterns. Men and women in little groups were dancing together to the music of concertinas, and gangs of youths were making nuisances of themselves by parading in long caterpillars and pushing their way, singing and shouting, through the throng. There was no traffic in Oxford Street, which was just as well, for it could not have moved;

'Dancing together to the music of concertinas'

the whole roadway was packed with people pushing slowly along, one way or the other, or coming to a stop in front of some particularly showy display.

It wasn't long before I, with my little legs, felt quite stifled down among the skirts of the crowd. I was lifted up on Father's shoulders, where I could get a splendid view of everything, but, what with the

86

day's excitement and all, I began to feel very sleepy and to nod. Mother saw this and said, 'Harry, I think it is time we went home.' No voice was raised in protest, and we began to fight our way out of

'I think it is time we went home'

the press. It took a long time to get clear and longer still to find a four-wheeler. Once safely inside, Cyril and I promptly fell asleep, and I was carried up to bed with the sounds of London celebrating getting ever fainter in my ears.

Chapter Five

WHITELEY'S FIRE

SCHOOL was very tedious after all the excitements of the Jubilee; and the end of term, though four weeks away, seemed an eternity ahead. The streets remained untidy with coloured paper and litter of all sorts, and we were told to be careful and look where we were going, as there was broken glass lying about where fairy lights had tumbled from window sills.

The Aunts' house had boasted a very modest decoration. Indeed, the atmosphere of respectability about Gordon Square seemed to prohibit much display. A few discreet flags were all that was considered proper.

We children went to see them on a Sunday in July. We went from Baker Street to Gower Street by Underground, the stuffiest and most unpleasant stretch of line it was possible to imagine, especially at that time of the year. The trains—steamers!—were dirty and were drawn by engines with two quite small extra funnels, one on each side, in addition to the one at the front. I asked a porter what these were for, and he told me that in the worst ventilated parts of the tunnel the driver could cut off the smoke and divert it through the water tanks. These were carried on either side of the boiler like a saddle, and therefore the engines were called tank engines. I would watch the trains approaching to see if the smoke were coming in puffs from the two small funnels, but it did not seem to make any difference to the atmosphere. From Gower Street to

Baker Street it was almost unbearable. Along the pavements of Euston Road, and in the middle of the road as well, were gratings through which some of the smoke found its way out. Standing on a grating, it was all hot and choking, and women never stood on them because the draught blew their skirts up.

The trains had three classes of accommodation, first, second, and

'Stuffiest and most unpleasant'

third. Some of the third-class seats were just wooden boards, with low partitions between, over which it was fun to steeplechase if there were not many passengers. When the train started from a station there was always a porter at the front end whose job it was to shut the doors. He did this with great skill, 'BANG!' 'BANG!' 'BANG!' as the train gathered speed, and he had to turn the handles too! The guard, after showing his green light and blowing his whistle, would wait for his van, then step on it as it sped past and swing himself inside, all very neatly done. We did not go very often by Underground, it was much nicer by bus.

None of our Aunts saw the Jubilee Procession, but Aunt Fanny firmly went to see the illuminations. She did so in spite of Aunt Alicia's protests and warnings that if she were not crushed or set on fire she would most certainly have her pocket picked. She and Mary the maid had sallied forth together and, to judge by the description that Aunt Fanny gave us, they had a whale of a time. They went everywhere and saw everything, and, short of dancing in the street, seemed to have joined in all the gaiety. They did not get home till midnight.

During the afternoon we spent with them we were told of the Aunts' plans for the summer, which were to stay at Highgate. They always took their summer holidays within driving distance of London, as Aunt Annie, being an invalid, could not stand long journeys, and Aunt Alicia, my godmother, had an abiding horror of trains, and more especially of tunnels. So a residence had to be found which had ten bedrooms and could be reached by horse-drawn vehicles. This year it was the Vicarage at Highgate, a pleasant house with a big garden.

All preparations were made, and, at the appointed time, Father took us along to bid the Aunts good-bye and to see them safely off. A private bus with two horses was hired, and this duly arrived at 53 Gordon Square. There it was loaded up with boxes of linen and enough stores to feed an army. Also there was Aunt Annie's invalid couch and chair, Aunt Fanny's knitting machine, four maids, two cages of canaries, and, finally, two Aunts. Aunt Fanny, alert and confident, was in supreme command, giving sharp orders to the driver while he staggered in and out of the house with the heavy boxes. She carried a little notebook and checked off the various items as they were put on board. Her skirts were girded up with strange snap fasteners, showing a pair of very neat ankles and tiny feet. She had everything under control.

Aunt Emily, on the other hand, darted in and out of the house

'Aunt Fanny . . . in supreme command'

in a state of semi-bewilderment, to see that the canaries were being handled carefully. It seemed that she had appeared, hot and fussed, fully dressed for the journey, at breakfast, though the pilgrimage was timed for 2 o'clock. A closed fly had been ordered for the two remaining Aunts, and this arrived while the loading up was in progress. Aunt Annie, the invalid, was helped in and made comfortable with cushions, while Aunt Alicia, well wrapped up, settled alongside. Finally, Jane the parlourmaid and Mrs Low the nurse were packed in. Some controversy arose over the transport of George, Mrs Low's canary. This was eventually settled by Aunt Fanny, who as chief organizer was called in to adjudicate, and the cage, with George fluttering wildly, was wrested from his protesting mistress and placed with the others in the bus.

When we heard that the journey was safely accomplished, Father went to Highgate to see the Aunts. He told us that their bus had had some difficulty in negotiating the climb up Highgate Hill, and that the horses had had to be stopped at one point. It appears that the man beside the driver got down and put the drag behind the wheel to prevent, as he said, the bus from running backwards. To start again was not an easy matter, and, on Aunt Fanny's suggestion, the maids and two Aunts got out. Aunt Fanny, in travelling array, with skirts girded up, boldly started to push. At this, some bystanders joined in, and, encouraged by cheers and their combined efforts, the bus started again. The Aunts and maids were unceremoniously bundled in while the vehicle was moving. Aunt Emily, much out of breath, barked her shin on the step. This, and the rough manner in which she had been handled, put her in a bad temper, which was not improved when they arrived at the Vicarage to find the fly waiting in the drive with the other travellers. It had taken an easier route and so had arrived first.

The house was open, but the only person who appeared to be about was a gardener. He, however, was able to assist them to get Aunt Annie, faint and weary, inside and into an easy chair. With the arrival of the bus-load of luggage Aunt Fanny was able to introduce order, and tempers were further soothed when crockery was unpacked and tea provided.

Father brought us an invitation to go and spend a day there, and he arranged that this should be a week or so later. It was a Saturday. I wore a clean white sailor blouse with a new straw hat which was very stiff and uncomfortable because the elastic cut my chin.

We went by bus to the bottom of Highgate Hill. It was very hot waiting for the cable tram, and Mother took us across the road to a shop and bought us some lemonade. Cyril and I were very interested in the cable trams. They ran on lines, and we could see one coming down the hill while the other was going up. There must have been some sort of cable under the street that kept moving, up one side and down the other, and the tram had a thing that gripped it. When one tram came to a stop at the bottom we ran forward to investigate the underside, and I was only stopped from crawling below by an agonized cry from Mother, 'Ernest! Your clothes!' Once on board, we could sit either in the open-sided compartment, or, which was better, on top, but both were very jolty. Near the top of the hill we passed under an archway high above the road, which Father said carried water.

The Vicarage smelt very much the same as Gordon Square. After greeting our Aunts we were allowed to run out in the garden. This had distinct possibilities, though much of it was tidy, with a tennis lawn and round beds with red, yellow, and blue flowers in neat rows. However, there were certain more remote places among bushes and rather untidy rockeries where one could lurk without fear of interruption from Aunts or gardeners.

Some people had been invited for the afternoon to play tennis, but then it was discovered that there was no machine for marking out the court, because, the gardener explained, the vicar did not like whitewash on the lawn. However, Father, full of resource, suggested that if yards and yards of white tape could be provided, together with plenty of hairpins, he would be able to mark the court out. Cyril and I were able to help him do this, and the lines were stretched and pegged down with hairpins. This worked well, unless of course you caught your foot in the tape, as happened to the curate during the course of the afternoon.

'Gay in a blue spotted dress'

The visitors began to arrive about three o'clock, some of them carrying tennis racquets and shoes, and there was animation and chatter upon the lawn. Aunt Emily was gay in a blue spotted dress and a large straw hat; though rather stout, she was able and ready to enjoy the game; in fact it was her suggestion that lawn tennis, rather than croquet, should be played.

Among the guests was a boy who came with the people from next door. He was a quiet youth, very shy, and seemed rather lost among the crowd. Mother found him looking at the lines in a rather bewildered fashion, and he asked her what they were for. She explained the game to him, and then, noticing his black hair, and that he spoke with a foreign accent, asked him about himself. He was Chinese, he explained, and was staying with friends in England. Mother promptly rounded up Cyril and me and introduced us. Willie—for that was his name, at least it was that in English; in Chinese it was something much longer—was older than we were; he had long trousers, and his suit was made of some light silky-

'Watched him cut and shape some little frogs'

looking material. He spoke in a queer high-pitched voice, and sometimes had to stop and think of the right word, but all the same he was very friendly and told us stories about China. For myself, I could not believe that he was really Chinese because he had no pigtail, and I asked him about it. Very sadly he answered that it had been cut off and that he had mourned many days. When he talked about China he smiled, and his eyes seemed to disappear. He said that, though he liked being in England, he wanted to go back to his own country. We found a quiet spot behind the rockery and sat there while he talked to us. Presently he said he could make toys with paper, so I went indoors and fetched some and a pair of scissors, and we watched him cut and shape some little frogs. He had very delicate and deft hands, and it was fascinating to watch him cutting and folding the paper. The frogs, when finished and pressed on their backs, jumped most effectively. We were sorry when the time came for him to go. We would have liked to have seen him again, but we never did.

When the tea bell rang, the tennis players trooped indoors, mopping their brows and discussing the games. The curate received much sympathy about his fall, and there was a lot of concern over the green stain on his trouser leg. We boys had to 'make ourselves useful' at tea time, carrying things—cups of tea or plates of cakes to those who preferred to sit outside—so that we could not do full justice to the meal ourselves and were glad when we could get back to the rockery and play with the frogs.

It was quite late when the time came to go home. Dusk was falling and in the drawing-room the lamps had been lit. We said 'good-bye' to the Aunts and remembered to thank them nicely. It was hot and close, and there was a queer light in the sky.

As we came to the top of Highgate Hill a lot of people were gathered, talking and pointing down the hill towards London, where a great red fan of light showed above the houses. They said there was a big fire burning down there, and all were wondering where it was. Gripping Mother's hand, I had the terrifying thought that it might be our house, and it was not until we boarded the cable tram

'A great red fan of light showed above the houses'

and the driver told us it was Whiteley's shop in Westbourne Grove that my fears were partially allayed. Still, fires have a way of spreading, and one could never be sure. . . . People on the tram were all talking about it, and when we reached the bottom of the hill I almost forgot my fears when a fire engine went dashing by, brass helmets

7   97

and all, with a fireman standing beside the driver shouting 'Clear the way—clear the way!' The engine had three horses, one in front of the other pair, and Father said that the extra horse showed it must have come a long way.

We had to wait for a bus, and all the time the fierce glow seemed to get stronger. When a bus finally arrived it was quite dark.

The glow got stronger and stronger as we neared Camden Town. People were running about and shouting as if the fire were in

'Clear the way!'

the next street. I kept asking: 'Can't we go home quickly?' At last Mother turned to Father and said, 'Harry, do see if you can find a cab.' There was an empty four-wheeler standing outside a public house on the corner, so Father boldly entered the place and came out with the cabman, who, wiping his mouth, reluctantly agreed to drive us to Kent Terrace. We drove round the Park and the glow looked terribly close as we reached the top of Park Road. It was a great relief to come in sight of our house and to find that all was well, with Martha and Lizzie standing outside the front door and all the maids gossiping by the area steps. There was a distant sound of throbbing and roaring and a smell of burning in the air. Our own policeman was making his way slowly along the Terrace, being stopped and asked for news as he did so. When he came to us he said the fire had been burning for hours, that there were forty fire engines at work, and that people had been turned out of their houses owing to the heat and the fear of the fire spreading. He gave us a piece of charred wood he had picked up in Park Road.

'The smell of burning came in strongly'

It had been a long day and I was very sleepy, but I did not want to go to bed. I was packed off there, of course, but not to sleep. Cyril came up soon afterwards, and we lay watching the red flickering light through the crack in the side of the blind. Then we got out of bed and went to the window, which was wide open, and the smell of burning came in strongly on the night air. I confided my

99

fears about fires spreading. Cyril pointed down the Terrace to where our policeman was still talking with the maids. Then only did I feel safe enough to go back to bed. But it was not till Mother came to tell us that she and Father had been out to see the fire, and had been quite near to it, and that it was a long, long way off, did I go to sleep.

It was some days before we boys were allowed to go to West-bourne Grove to see the scene of the conflagration. This was because the postman had told Martha that there was a danger of the walls falling. I kept worrying Mother until she said we might go, but not too near, and Martha was to keep us by her. Ethel agreed to come with us, but I fancy this was really because she, and Martha too, wanted to see the shops in Praed Street.

Before the Great Central Line and Marylebone Station were built, one could walk straight across from Kent Terrace, up Alpha Place, past Boscobel Place, and, crossing Lisson Grove and Edgware Road, come to Westbourne Grove. Having done this we found a barrier across the road, but by worming our way to the front we could see quite a lot. A salvage engine, the men wearing black leather helmets, was standing near. Further down was a real fire engine with some hoses stretching up and down the street. Someone said the fire was still smouldering down in the basement. The long front of the shop was a sorry sight, with part of the wall fallen and the rest blackened, with gaping windows, and charred wood and broken glass littering the roadway.

Some men were putting up a hoarding at the far end. We watched it all, and listened to the people in the crowd. One woman was telling how she and her children had been turned out in the night because they feared that the fire would spread across the street, and how the house fronts all down their road had been scorched and blistered and the windows broken with the heat. Then they talked of the firemen who had been injured, and of one poor fellow who had been killed when a beam fell and crushed his brass helmet.

'The long front of the shop was a sorry sight'

It was some time before we could be dragged away, and when we started for home we boys were sent on alone, Martha and Ethel making for Praed Street.

Off the Edgware Road we took a narrow street filled with barrows selling vegetables and fruit, rabbits and fish. It was thronged with shoppers. At the far end, before turning into Lisson Grove, we saw, up a side street, a crowd gathering and people running. It was not a wise thing to do, but we went to investigate.

'Threw herself on the policeman'

As we came near we saw a policeman struggling with a man. The policeman was not a big man, but he seemed to be very strong. Even so he was not able to hold the other fellow, who was far bigger than he. The man had a red choker handkerchief round his neck, and the policeman managed to get hold of this and twist it. This made the man lash out with his fists, and shout, 'Yer chokin' me!' Just then a woman began to scream, and the crowd parted, as she ran in and threw herself on the policeman. She kept crying out: 'They shan't take you! They shan't take you! Bill, don't let them take you!'

The crowd surged backwards and forwards and Cyril and I were forced against some wooden palings, where we stood, both very frightened but fascinated. There was a young woman farther down the street with a baby in her arms. She kept moaning and sobbing, and between her sobs she repeated, ''E 'asn't done nothing,' and ''E's been a good man to me.'

Nobody tried to help the policeman. His helmet had fallen off, and he and the man were now struggling on the ground. Both had blood on their faces. The officer wrenched his hand free for a moment and fumbled for his whistle. He had hardly got it to his mouth when the man hit him in the face. It was a cruel blow, for it crushed the whistle against his mouth. Nevertheless he blew it loudly before he had to give up as his mouth was all disfigured. With my back against the palings, I felt I was going to be sick; my hands and feet were quite cold, and I saw that Cyril's face was very white. Then, suddenly, the crowd began to melt away, for, running towards them, was an-other police-

'Felt I was going to be sick'

man. The woman tried to put herself in his way, but he brushed her aside and, as he came up, I saw him draw his truncheon from his hip. Neither Cyril nor I could look. We were close to the scene, but, frozen with terror and unable to run, we dared not turn and see what happened. We only knew that, soon after, the new policeman had the man by the choker and was dragging him up. The man kept struggling and shouting oaths and abuse, but they got him to his feet. It was a funny thing, but directly the other constable appeared, those of the crowd who had re-

'Uttering in a strident voice'

mained seemed to be on the side of law

and order. They went so far as to staunch the wounds of the damaged policeman and retrieve his helmet. Then the man was led off in a rather dazed condition, and the street began to settle down. But small groups formed around the door of a house at the lower end, where a woman was uttering in a strident voice a stream of unfavourable generalizations about the police force as a whole.

My impression of the fire, drawn at the age of seven

Cyril was leaning his head against the palings. I said: 'Are you all right? Do let's go home.'

It was some minutes before we moved, and we had to go the length of the street. Immediately we had turned the corner we began to run. By the time our breath had given out we were across Lisson Grove and almost within sight of home. I asked Cyril: 'Did the policeman hit him with his truncheon?'

'I don't know. I shut my eyes.'

'So did I, but he *can't* have hit him very hard.'

Then: 'Do you think the policeman will die?'

Cyril said 'No' in a rather uncertain voice. All the same, it was a difficult thing to answer.

As we turned the corner into Park Road, we saw, to our joy, our own policeman standing at the corner by the pillar box. We rushed up to him and poured forth a torrent of words, each trying to describe the fight. He listened to us patiently, and then said, 'Now, don't you young gentlemen go and poke your noses into things of that sort. Quite likely you'd get into trouble—serious trouble.'

Which, on the whole, was sound advice.

Chapter Six

POLLARD'S FARM

THE summer holidays were well advanced when we were told we were going with Father and Mother to stay at a farmhouse in Kent. We had been to the seaside several times, but had never been to the real country before, and Cyril and I were very excited at the prospect. I asked innumerable questions. The farm was called Pollard's.

'Mother, what is it like? Do they have cows?'

'Yes, darling, I expect there will be lots of cows, and we shall get nice fresh farmhouse butter.'

'But, Mother, the Dorset butter we have at home is salt and I don't like it.'

'Well, I'm sure the butter will be nice, and you'll have eggs all new laid, and perhaps home-made bread.'

'Ooh!' was all I could say to that. Then—'Mother, do they have rabbits as well as cocks and hens?'

'I expect so, and pigs as well, and they say there are hop fields, and if we stay long enough we can see them picking the hops. It is great fun; all the families in the neighbourhood come, children and all, and pick away all day. When Uncle Henry was Rector of Chiddingstone I stayed with them and we all went picking, and I remember how sore it made my fingers.'

It was afternoon when we climbed into the train at Charing Cross. Cyril and I always enjoyed a railway journey, though it was a pity we were not allowed to lean out of the windows. After stopping at a number of stations, we began to leave behind the little houses and chimneys of the outskirts of London and the afternoon sun shone on fields and lanes. Before we reached our destination Father pointed out some hop fields. The hops were trained up poles, and Father explained how the poles were laid across canvas bags for the picking.

'Spread a tarpaulin cape over our shoulders'

Pollard's Farm was several miles from the station, and the porter who handled our luggage told us that the farm wagonette was waiting for us. There, sure enough, it was, with a youth, whom the porter called Charlie, standing by the horse's head. The luggage was piled on, and off we started. It had begun to rain a little, so Cyril and I, sitting on the box-seat, spread a tarpaulin cape over our shoulders.

As we went along, Charlie told us about the farm. He told us of a new litter of pigs, for one thing, and how Mrs Pollard had won a prize for bread at the village Show. It was all very new and exciting, especially when we came in sight of some queer-shaped, pointed roofs. 'They be oast houses,' Charlie told us, pointing with his whip, 'where they dry and pocket the hops. Like enough you'll see them doin' it—that is, if you're here at the right time.'

The road was getting muddy and the horse splashed in the puddles as we trotted along. Soon we turned into a narrow lane and saw ahead of us a red-tiled farmhouse. 'Pollard's,' said Charlie. At the end of the lane we passed through an open gate, and drove round to the back of the square-fronted farmhouse, pulling up in a spacious yard. A black-and-white rough-haired dog came out of his kennel with much rattling of his chain, and stood barking and waving his tail.

The farmhouse door was opened and a woman came out. She was very stout, with a cheerful red face. She greeted us in a friendly way, but when Father and Mother shook hands with her she was rather flustered. Wiping her hands on her apron first, she said ''Tis the flour, with me baking buns for the young people.' Cyril and I exchanged a quick look. 'Buns!'

We went in through a great kitchen where a small maid was trying to hide behind an enormous deal table. She bobbed a curtsey, and stood looking at us with her mouth open. Charlie carried in our luggage, and Cyril and I were sent upstairs to wash.

There was no bathroom, but washstands with white china jugs and basins were in the bedrooms, which were pervaded by a faint smell of camphor. We boys had a large room, the floor of which sloped, so that we felt we were going downhill when we went to the window. This had white dimity curtains. The bed, which we were to share, was very large and very soft to bounce on; there was a feather mattress in which we could feel the spikes of the feathers, when we pressed it, but it proved rather hot to sleep in. Below the window was a small, neat garden, and by looking sideways we could

'Wiping her hands on her apron'

see into the farmyard with its tiled roofs, and beyond could glimpse a wooden barn and some haystacks.

It did not take us long to wash and we ran along to have a look at Ethel's room. It was gayer than ours, with a spotted pink wallpaper and bright curtains, but was very small and grown-ups had to duck their heads under the doorway.

Lovely smells were now coming up from below as of sizzling bacon and eggs, and we clattered downstairs to the parlour, which was not often used but was now brushed up for the occasion. We were greeted by a delectable sight. The round table fairly groaned under the weight of good things. Plates loaded with buns, pots of

jam, a dish of yellow butter and a large plum cake. Then there was a great round loaf, and plates of biscuits and cheese, and bottles of pickles, and in fact everything you could think of. A great brown teapot was standing on a side table. Our eyes were goggling at it all when Mrs Pollard came in with a dish full of bacon and eggs. She said, proudly, "Tis home-cured, and I hope it will be enough.' Even Father's eyes sparkled and we boys hardly knew where to begin.

"Tis home-cured'

When the feast came to an end, and we had stuffed till we could stuff no more, Cyril and I lay back in our chairs. We had planned to explore the farm, but, overcome by drowsiness, decided to let that wait till tomorrow; anyhow it was growing dark. A lamp was brought in. Outside, the rain had stopped and there were distant farmyard sounds. It was all very peaceful. As I sat there a large moth flew in at the window and began to flutter round and round the lamp. I grew sleepier and sleepier. Father was reading the newspaper, and he looked up and said, 'Those boys ought to be in bed.' As this was exactly what I had been thinking, we went upstairs to our feather-bed without a murmur, and only Mother's reminder saved us from going to sleep without cleaning our teeth or saying our prayers.

When I woke up in the morning I could not for the life of me remember where I was. Strange, dark, oak beams across the ceiling, and whitewashed walls and, hanging over the washstand, an illuminated text in bright red and blue letters with convolvulus twirling round the words 'The Lord shall preserve thee and keep thee'. The dimity curtains were drawn, but it was light enough to see everything. I was sunk deep in the feather-bed, so that I could only see a bit of Cyril's shape alongside. It was fortunate that the bed was a big one, for he was apt to thresh about in the night. I pushed up my head and could see that he was still asleep.

By this time I had taken it all in, and could hear the farmyard noises outside; so I climbed out of bed and made the downhill journey to the window and pulled back the curtains, which were on large wooden rings. The clatter of these woke Cyril up, but he only said 'What?' and went to sleep again. The window was as high as my chin, so I got a chair, climbed on it and pushed open the casement. Last night's rain had made the ground smell nice, and a bright morning sun was shining. The garden plot below had a lavender hedge, and a brick path led round to the back of the house. Leaning out as far as I could, I saw that the farmyard was rapidly coming to life. Obviously now was the time to go and see what it was all about. So I woke Cyril, still very sleepy and protesting, and we struggled into our clothes.

It was very early, and before we ventured downstairs we stood listening intently on the landing. Nobody seemed to be stirring. We went downstairs to the square hall, where there were pegs on the wall with coats and hats hanging on them, and a gun standing in the corner. A big door promised a way out, but it had a heavy lock and the key would not turn, so we decided to try another way. There was another door, and this we pushed open. It led down two steps into the kitchen, which looked larger than ever in the morning sunshine. There were a lot of things we had not noticed the previous evening. There were hooks on the oak beams, and a kitchen range

'Pushed open the casement'

with gleaming brass knobs set in a chimney recess. A lavender-coloured frill hung on the mantel, which was quite high up, and above it was a wooden rack with a gun. There was an exciting square clock on the wall with a great round face and a picture of a volcano erupting in the centre. It ticked away loudly, and I asked Cyril to tell me the time, not being good at telling the time myself. It was five minutes past six.

There were pots of geraniums on the high window sill, with a tortoiseshell cat curled up between them where the sun made a splash. Cyril went across and stroked it—he was always fond of cats—and it got up, stretched itself, arched its back and purred. The clock ticked on slowly, and there was a faint buzzing of bees. It seemed as if nothing wanted to wake up.

The door into the yard was open and we went out. Beside the door were two brightly polished milk cans set upside down on posts. Across the yard we heard a man's voice. We

'Tortoiseshell cat curled up'

crossed over to a gateway, from where we could see the cowshed.

'Do you think they'd mind if we went in?'

'Come on, I'm sure it's all right.'

A roofed archway gave a glimpse of haystacks beyond and the sounds came from an open door. A man's voice kept saying 'Coom oop!' 'Coom oop!' and there was a swishing sound. Then out came Charlie. He was carrying two milk pails with a wooden yoke on his shoulders. He saw us and grinned, 'You'm oop early,' he said. 'Do 'e want to see the milkin'?' To our eager 'Yes!' he replied, 'Coom across then, but don't 'e go inside.'

We stood in the doorway, and saw that the cows were standing in rows inside, while an old man in a greasy felt hat, which was pressed against the flank of a cow, was sitting on a three-legged stool with a bright pail between his knees. He took no notice of us, but

8

made queer grunts and noises which the cows seemed to understand. The sound of the milk in the pail was strange and rather soothing.

'Do you think they'd mind if we went in?'

I asked Cyril if he thought we could have some milk as I was feeling very empty. 'Do you think, if we went back to the house, Mrs Pollard would give us some?' Cyril agreed it might be worth trying, so we crossed the yard again. The farmer's wife was by the door and saw us coming. 'Lor' bless 'e, 'tis early 'e are, and breakfast not for another hour! Come along in and have a bite of somethin'—but see and tidy yer boots!' she added, pointing to a broom scraper beside the door.

Our boots being satisfactorily tidied, we clattered in. 'Now sit 'e down,' said Mrs Pollard. We clambered on to chairs by the vast kitchen table and watched with eager eyes while she fetched a jug of milk and two cups. Then out came one of the round loaves, and large slices of bread and butter were cut. We both remembered to say 'Thank you!' before our mouths were full, and while we munched away I thought what a wonderful place a farm was.

'I reckon you don't get such fare in Lunnon,' said Mrs Pollard.

'It's much better than porridge,' was all that I could think of in reply. 'And I like bacon and eggs and sausages, too.'

She laughed heartily at this. 'Well, there won't be no stint o' them here,' she said, 'but mind 'e don't go spoiling your breakfast.'

'What is there for breakfast?' I was saying, when Cyril kicked me under the table.

It was close on eight o'clock when Mother came down and found us in the front garden. We had already been across the yard and made friends with the black-and-white dog whose name was Chance. He stood up and put his paws on our shoulders and never stopped wagging his tail. Now we were grubbing in the soil to make a grotto with some stones and our hands were filthy, so we were sent upstairs to clean ourselves before being allowed to sit down to breakfast. It *was* eggs and bacon, *and* fried bread, and Mrs Pollard gave us a broad grin as she brought the dish in.

Ethel joined us boys after the meal, and we went exploring all

'We both remembered to say "Thank you"'

round the farm. We soon found that no one seemed to mind where we went. The cowman, who was also the pig man, warned us to keep away from the palings round the sty, for the old sow was not

too good-tempered and had been known to
bite. There was a black hen in the yard with
one foot missing. It had been bitten off by the
sow, so the pig man said. The hen got about
quite nimbly on one leg, but we were much concerned for her and made a special bed of straw
in a corner by the barn, but she scorned this,
preferring to roost with her fellows. Later on
she became much attached to me, and would
follow us indoors and even try to mount the
stairs. Unknown to Father and Mother, I carried her upstairs and she spent several nights in
our bedroom; until one evening, going up after
we were asleep, Mother discovered her com-
fortably tucked up in bed between us. And that was the end of that.

'I carried her upstairs'

'Tucked up in bed between us'

117

There was much to do on fine days, and when it was raining we climbed the ladder in the barn. We had discovered that there was a little door by the hay-loft, which gave access to the place above the archway. It was very small, but if we kept low and minded the cobwebs, it made a wonderful hiding place. By peering through the cracks in the floor, we could look down on anyone passing below and we felt we were in a castle. Altogether most romantic!

Ethel had too much respect for her clothes to venture up there, but she would join us on the straw of the loft and tell us stories. I say 'stories' but it was really one story that went on and on, from holiday to holiday, winter and summer, and could be embellished and ornamented with all sorts of ideas and suggestions. Ethel was a great reader and seemed to have an endless fund of knowledge. We all became kings and queens in her story, and our friends were suitably rewarded with titles. I made a point of trying to draw everything, and would illustrate some of the more exciting passages; especially when, bowing to popular demand, Ethel allowed our combined armies to be described on their return from battle in triumph, after a shattering defeat of the common enemy, all drawn in detail. I always had several odds and ends of paper stuffed inside my sailor tunic, and these were filled with drawings. I used a pencil because that was easier to carry about, and though the point got broken pretty often, it could be sharpened, if Father were handy, with a knife; failing that, it could be bitten with the teeth till the lead showed, though the resulting point was not a very good one.

The cowman's name was Ned. He told us that he had worked for Mr Pollard's father, and that the farm had belonged to the Pollard family for ages and ages; there was no knowing how long they *had* owned it. He told us that his old Dad used to work near by, and remembered before the railway came, when all had to travel by wagon. The workers were paid very little money but were given their milk and bread and wood for firing, and when pigs were killed they had their share of the pork, which was salted and kept the year round in a barrel.

'Join us on the straw of the loft and tell us stories'

Charlie was a never-failing source of information. He told us all about the beasts and birds and seasons, and where we could go, and where we couldn't. Then there were the haystack men, who generally seemed to be on top of something. One of them (another Charlie, which was confusing, but he had red hair to make things easier) talked all the time and cracked jokes at the others.

The village was half a mile away from the farm. There was one shop which seemed to sell everything one could possibly want. It

'She chose a pink one'

had jars of sweets on shelves, pails and brushes, saucepans, fly-papers and mousetraps hanging from beams. By the door-posts were strong hobnailed boots and coconut matting. A display of millinery at the back included some brightly coloured country bonnets. But the fireworks left over from last year were damp and wouldn't go off.

One morning we went there in the wagonette with Mother, and Ethel was allowed to choose a country bonnet. She chose a pink one and tied it on with the strings under her chin. Both Cyril and I agreed that it was an improvement on the rather floppy straw thing that she usually wore. We were looking, rather wistfully, at the glass jars of sweets when the shopwoman told us that the big bull's eyes were made by an old man who lived in the village. He had a tiny cottage up the lane, and made all kinds of sweets. This was exciting news, and we begged Mother to take us there. So off we went up the lane, and came to a little cottage with a tidy garden in front. There was no other cottage in sight, so this must be it. The door was open and Mother looked in. She said, 'Good morning.' An old man appeared in his shirtsleeves. He had curly white hair and a beard. Mother said 'Good morning' again, and then 'I hear you make sweets, Mr Er—Er——'

'Bin makin' them for over twenty year, ever since the old lady died, but it ain't so easy to get the things as it war.'

'May the children see you making them?' Mother asked.

The old man considered this, and then said slowly, 'Coom along o' Monday afternoon I'll be makin',' he went on, 'an' maybe I can show 'em how 'tis done.'

'Oh, thank you very much, Mr Er—Er.' So it was arranged, and we went off in high glee, and called him Mr Er—Er— for ever afterwards.

On Sunday morning Mother took us to church. The congregation included a lot of people from the village in their best clothes, the women in tight shiny black bodices and straw bonnets or hats, and some of the older men, Mr Er—Er— among them, in clean white smocks. Mr Er—Er—'s outfit was completed by a rusty top hat. There was a mixed choir, but not in surplices, and the singing was led by a clerk with a strident voice which rather drowned the organ, but as the latter was a bit wheezy it didn't much matter.

The rest of Sunday was rather dull. No one seemed to be around. The cows came drowsing in to be milked, the bees droned, and it was all very sleepy. Cyril and I wandered about the farm. We leant over the half-door of the stables, where the big horses were, and I watched the flies go in and out and worry the poor beasts. I thought they would have been happier in the fields, where they could stand

'In their best clothes'

end to end and swish each other with their tails, as I had seen them doing. We longed for Monday.

When it came, Father had to go to London, so the wagonette was got out to take him to the station, and it dropped us children at the corner of the lane. Old Mr Er—Er— was at work in his cottage, surrounded by pots and pans. Something was boiling on the fire and there was a smell of hot sugar. He had a lump of sticky stuff which he was kneading. 'Sit 'e down and watch,' he said, 'whilst I does the

pullin'.' There was a bright iron hook fixed to the rafters, and he stretched the sweet stuff over it and then pulled and pulled. Over and over again he pulled and turned and folded it and then pulled again, till it began to grow bright and shiny. Then he turned and wound it with a thin brown ribbon of sweet, cutting it into short lengths with scissors over a tin box. He gave us a sly glance. 'Ever 'eared o' bull's eyes?' he said. 'I reckon they're bigger nor you get in Lunnon.' He handed

'Sit 'e down and watch'

us each one. They were quite hot and filled our mouths. He showed us bottles and cans with other sweets. Mother had given us some money, so we were able to choose quite a lot for one shilling and ninepence. Before we left he took us into his garden and showed us some of the sweet herbs that he used to flavour his sweets. We had a lot to tell Mother when we got back to the farm.

The following day, when Father came back from London, he told us that someone who went to our school had mumps and that we could not go back to school for a fortnight or more. We could therefore stay on at the farm. This joyous news meant that we should be able to see the hop-picking, which would begin in a day or two, the gipsies having already begun to arrive; their carts had been seen on the roads.

The gipsies camped in a corner of the field. The camp was very untidy, with a bad-tempered, growly dog, and we were told not to go there; but it was difficult to resist, for the gipsies were very friendly. One woman offered to tell my fortune, but I hadn't got a silver sixpence, so I never knew what my fortune was to be. The hop field was close to the farm. *Too* close to the orchard, said Mrs Pollard, and we wondered why, till one day, early in the morning, we heard a rumpus and were told that 'they folk were stealing the apples'.

When picking began we went to the field with Mother and Edith, the little maid, who wasn't a bit shy when she got out of doors. Her young brother joined us, but he was very disobedient and rather a nuisance. How different the field looked now! It was crowded with pickers sitting round the long canvas troughs, whilst the men pulled down the poles and laid them handy. Whole family parties were at work, with their dinners packed in baskets or tied up in handkerchiefs. The gipsy folk kept aloof in their picking and did not mingle with the others. We were told that all were paid according to the amount they picked, so it was an advantage to have a large family. At intervals a man would come along and empty the canvas troughs, keeping a tally in a book, and at the end of the day the farmer who owned the field paid for the day's work. He grinned when he came to us, and gave each of us a shilling. It was wonderful to have so much money, and I couldn't decide whether to spend it on the sweet man, or marry Vera Beringer, which I had wanted to do ever since I had been taken to see her act *Little Lord Fauntleroy*. It was the first money I had really earned, and it was to be a long time before I earned any more. Mother had been right about hop picking making our fingers sore, and the smell made our eyes water as well.

We went to the farm for our dinner, but returned to the field

'Followed the cart out of the gate'

afterwards, and picked till we could pick no more. When the canvas bags were full they were piled on a cart and driven to the oast house. Charlie was driving the cart in the afternoon, and asked us if we would like to go with him to the oast house. So we followed the cart out of the gate, all three of us, and raced up the road. Running as hard as we were able we could not keep up with Charlie. Cyril, very hot and breathless, came second, I followed (explaining loudly that my brother was two years older than I). Ethel was a long way behind, although she was the eldest, because she kept stopping to pull up her stockings.

The man at the oast house said he was too busy to answer all our questions, but that if we came another day he would show us how

'Dan lowered himself in'

the hops were dried and packed. The inside of the oast house looked very interesting, and Cyril and I were impatient till the day came and we were allowed to go off in the morning. We ran all the way. The oast house was a round building with a pointed roof and ladders leading to the top. It was divided into floors. The hops were dried by being spread on a sort of wire frame. A man with a wooden rake kept turning them over and over. Down below some small fires were burning with a blue flame; these were fed with yellow stuff which the man, on being questioned, said was sulphur. It made my throat tingle. Presently, when the hops were dry enough, they were gathered up and taken to another floor. This had a round hole in the middle, with a great long sack fixed in it. 'We calls that the pocket,' said the man. 'An' you watch how we presses 'em. Dan!' he called, 'are 'e ready?' Dan had a very old felt hat with a wide brim, which he turned down so that you could only see the lower part of his face. Then they tipped some hops into the long sack, and Dan lowered

'To see things from below'

himself in after them, slowly disappearing, until only the top of his hat could be seen. ''E does the treadin',' explained the man, and Dan began to tread, working round and round, while more hops were poured in over his head.

Gradually Dan began to reappear, very unkempt and dusty: first his hat, then his shoulders; as more hops were poured in he rose higher and higher. Cyril and I kept climbing down the ladder to see things from below. The sack shook and vibrated as Dan trod. It hung from the ceiling like a big cocoon. At last it was full, and Dan stepped out and shook himself. He was covered with bits of hop, but he didn't seem to mind. 'Bin' doin' it for twenty-five year,' said the man. 'Twenty-nine, come next pickin',' corrected Dan. When the pocket was full it was sewn up with a carpet needle. Then it was lifted off by a pulley, and was ready to go away to be made into beer.

We were covered with dust, and thoroughly grimy when we got back to the farm for dinner, and our throats tingled for days.

It was only a few days later that Father returned from London and reported that the mumps were over and that we must go home. I felt very sad at leaving the farm. I wandered round saying good-bye to the horses, and the little pigs, to Charlie and to Chance, and to the little lame hen. In the kitchen we all drank dandelion wine, and Mr Pollard was quite jovial. He was a silent man, as a general rule, whom we had hitherto seen only at a distance. We thanked Mrs Pollard, who asked us to come again, and said, if we liked, she could supply us with fresh eggs from the farm. Edith, behind the kitchen table, quite forgot to curtsey; she ran to the gate and stood there, a forlorn little figure, in tears, as the wagonette took us to the station.

On the whole it was nice to be back home again. Martha, all smiles, opened the front door. The fire was burning in the dining-room, and Lizzie had prepared a very particular tea with crumpets. Sambo joined us, purring and fussing round us all. Father and Mother had a lot of letters to read, and we children sat back feeling very comfortable and content. The trees outside were beginning to turn, and the old messenger man was sweeping up the leaves. Presently the lamplighter, with his staff, came along the Terrace, and one by one the lamps were lit. It really *was* rather nice to be home once more.

Chapter Seven

BELOW STAIRS

O**UR** kitchen was a comfortable place, especially on chill autumn afternoons. A large range occupied one end, with a coal fire burning cheerfully. There was a square deal table with Sambo's milk saucer beneath, and four or five windsor chairs grouped round it. On special occasions we children had tea in the kitchen with Lizzie and Martha. As we sat at the table, which was covered with a white cloth, we could look up and see outside the window the bottom of the area railings and the legs of the passers-by. When it was dark, the kitchen was lit by a gas bracket over the table.

'Always wore black kid gloves'

Every Thursday Lizzie's sisters, Esther and Mary Ann, came to tea. They both had fringes and wore black dresses, Esther's being the grander, with shiny black bugles down the front. She always wore black kid gloves, which made it awkward when eating hot buttered toast. When tea was over and the things cleared away, the black kid gloves would be carefully wiped.

Then would follow some family gossip between the sisters. Mary Ann had a piece of embroidery which seemed never-ending. She kept it in a duster, which she would spread on her knees. Once

9   129

she showed us boys how to thread a needle without getting the cotton all black. She always bit off the ends of cotton on her stitchery, and this caused strong protests from Martha, who warned her of the fate which overtook a woman of whom her own mother had heard, who as a result of indulging in this practice, died suddenly in

'The large tin roaster'

agonies. Post mortem examination showed that the ends of cotton had got wound round her heart and strangled her!

Now came the time for the fire to be made up in preparation for 'late dinner' upstairs. If it were to be a roast joint, the large tin roaster would be brought in from the scullery. This was a round tin box, standing on legs, with an open front, and a door at the back through which you could peep to see how the meat was roasting. There was a wind-up thing at the top which turned slowly round, with the joint on a hook. When loaded, it was pushed close to the front of the open kitchen range, and soon the fat began to sizzle and drip into the pan below, and smell good.

On the whole there was little conversation, except when Martha was there, and what with the tea and hot toast and all I was apt to get sleepy. But Martha did brighten things up, especially since she had been 'walking-out' with her 'young man', as she called him. She had known him for a long time, but, as he lived far away in the west of England, she only saw him when she went on holiday. That summer, when she returned, she told Mother, in some confusion, that they were engaged. She was so shy that all Mother could get out of her was: 'He is a very nice man. He is a guard on the line.'

This was of course great news for Cyril and me, for a guard ranked high with us, next after a soldier or a fireman, and we were very anxious to meet him. We could not understand why Martha

'A grand exhibition of how the points worked'

called him her 'Young Man', for in the photos she showed us he had a beard and did not look young. She told us that, when she got married, they were going to live near her mother's home in Gloucestershire. She also said that her 'intended' was going to receive a rise and work on the passenger trains. Thus he would be able to get a pass to London, and in fact was coming to see her soon. So it was arranged that he should be invited to tea.

He duly arrived, very shy, with Martha shyer still, and blushing a lot. But, alas! he was not in uniform. This might have spoilt the whole afternoon; but, after tea, when shyness had worn off, he was persuaded to talk about trains. He explained endless technical matters to do with signals and points and engines, and then gave a grand exhibition of how the points worked by emptying his match box on to the table and laying the matches out like lines. He asked Martha if he could smoke a pipe. 'Would the Missus mind if he did?' On being reassured, he lit up—a highly interesting and novel process for us, for neither Father nor any of our uncles smoked.

Altogether it was a most successful afternoon, hallowed by a vague hint that it might be possible to get the young gentlemen a ride on an engine if they came down West.

'Sitting in her easy chair'

Cyril and I liked to go down to the kitchen of an afternoon, when our parents were out and Martha had taken Ethel to her music lesson or to a rehearsal of the Toy Symphony, which was to be performed later at the Lloyds', along the Terrace. Lizzie would be sitting in her easy chair, and would tell us how she came to be Mother's nurse when she herself was only seventeen and Grandma no more than twenty-two. Grandma had married an artist named William Lee when she was sixteen. He was a water-colour painter, and much older than she was, and had died many years before this story begins.

Mother could only just remember him, but Lizzie would tell us about the house in Torrington Square, where Grandma lived and so many artists and actors forgathered.

Grandma had a very good voice and used to sing ballads, some-

132

times at the Crystal Palace, and she knew Arthur Sullivan, and Lizzie said, 'I always thought that Mr Sullivan was sweet on your Mamma.' Lizzie had always been fond of the theatre, and became a regular first-nighter. Father encouraged her to go, as, he said, she was the best critic he knew. She always spoke of Ellen Terry as 'Miss Ellen', for the actress had been a friend of Grandma's, and was often at the house. Then there was 'Young Mr Robertson' (Johnston Forbes-Robertson) who came too, rather stiff and shy, so Lizzie said.

I can remember one party that was given at Kent Terrace when I was very small. Cyril, Ethel and I had been sent to bed, but we crept downstairs in our nightclothes and looked through the banisters at the fun. It was a lively scene, with the ladies in their gay coloured evening dresses with neat little waists and bustles. Many of the men wore white gloves, and had flowers in their buttonholes. Mother worked hard to make the party a success and seemed to be everywhere at once. A white drugget had been laid over the drawing-room carpet which made the room look twice the size. It would have made a perfect subject for Tissot. There was no dancing, but Hayden Coffin sang, and a small woman tinkled on the guitar. Then Beerbohm Tree recited, but Cyril and I were much more interested in the pretty ladies. One had dark, almost black hair and a red velvet dress. She had lovely white shoulders. Looking up and seeing our faces through the banisters, she laughingly chided us. Then she came up and, sitting on the stairs beside me, said, 'Why, Ernest, you are half asleep!' Which I was, so I promptly cuddled up to her. I had to be carried up to bed, where she tucked me up and gave me such a comforting kiss.

There was more that Lizzie told us. She said that when Father and Mother were first married and lived in the little house in Boscobel Place, they were fond of having some of their closest friends in to supper on Sunday evenings: Grandma was often there, and so were the Dicksees. Polly, Minnie and Frank Dicksee had been friends since childhood, so they were old friends of Lizzie's too. She told us how, in the summer evenings, the guests would sit in the tiny garden after supper while Mother played and sang. Sometimes Grandma sang

'Why, Ernest, you are half asleep!'

too. Aunt Fanny occasionally hazarded the journey from Gordon Square (leaving Aunt Alicia in deep concern till she returned home).

When Mother's babies came and it was no longer easy for her to entertain at home, she and Father more often went to the Sunday evening gatherings at the Dicksees' large house in Fitzroy Square. This had two studios, one for Minnie and one for her father Thomas Dicksee, with a connecting corridor lined with classical statuary.

Frank had his studio in Campden Hill. As we children grew older, first Ethel, then Cyril and I, were invited too. We always enjoyed going; for one thing it was a treat to sit up to supper with the grown-ups, and then, most interesting people, musical and artistic, were frequently there. The Dicksees had a small niece, with the same name as my sister. Little Ethel sometimes stayed with them. She was younger than I was and though I did not see her often, we were great friends. I was more than ever delighted to go to Fitzroy Square when she was there.

She was very pretty, with dark brown hair and a dear little snub nose, and the most expressive eyes. We had plenty to talk about—our respective schools and the parties we had been to. We sat together on the sofa, or on little stools by the fire, with our arms round each other, and listened to the conversation among the grown-ups. Or perhaps it was stories about Uncle Remus and Brer Rabbit and Brer Fox, told to us by Florence Reason, an artist friend who was often there. She could always be persuaded to come to a quiet corner of the room and entertain us.

I was most interested when the conversation was about art or music. I remember old Signor Garcia telling us about his experiences as an opera singer at the time Queen Victoria came to the throne. He had sung at Covent Garden many times, and then turned his attention to teaching. Most of the famous singers of the time were taught by him. On one occasion Minnie Dicksee asked him if he had ever sung with Jenny Lind. He considered a moment. 'No,' he said. 'No, you see I left the operatic stage in eighteen forty.'

Quite a different type of visitor was old Dr Gregory. A confirmed bachelor, small, stout and quite bald, he reminded me of Mr Pickwick. He always wore a well-cut frock coat made from the finest broadcloth, which, as the buttons failed to meet, was held together

over his paunch by a cuff-link. He had a special frock coat for the
cold weather lined with brown fur that smelt strongly of camphor.
He had very short legs so that, sitting on a chair, his feet barely
reached the ground. He wore elastic-sided boots with square toes,
and was very proud of his small feet, which were certainly beautifully shod. He was a great character and very argumentative. The
most harmless statement would be met with 'Well, I don't know
——' Then he would start off on a long list of reasons why this or
that were not so, or were so. He was inclined to be censorious about
people and places. For some reason he had a down on Stroud in
Gloucestershire. 'Nothing good ever came from *that place*,' he would
say. Even to mention it made him fume. He was great on hygiene,
and had an abhorrence of long hair in men; he would refer to
'close-cropped men like myself' as being superior; there was not a
hair on his head. His partiality for hygiene made him intolerant of
anybody with a spotty face. 'No right to be like that,' he would say,
and rumour had it that the one romance of his life was wrecked by
the object of his affections sweating too freely.

If any subject to do with doctoring was raised he would give the
company a full analysis of the causes and symptoms of each ailment.
Little Ethel and I sat in fear and trembling and clutching each other
even more tightly, as we thought of all the diseases we might have.
With me the fear was not a possibility but became a certainty as I
brooded over symptoms after going to bed. I would wake up with,
perhaps, a pain in my leg. This meant that the limb would have to
be cut off, a grim thought, and I wondered if little Ethel would like
me any longer if I had to go about with a wooden leg. Finally, unable to bear the suspense any longer I confided my fears to Lizzie,
who took a very practical view of things and assured me I was only
suffering from 'Growing Pains'.

Lizzie was always most interested in our prattle about the people we had met at Fitzroy Square, and would remind us before we went there to give her best respects to Miss Polly and Miss Minnie. They remembered her at Christmas, sending her some gaily decorated calendar. She possessed a reproduction of one of Frank's pictures, in which he had painted Mother, hanging in the kitchen.

'Close-cropped men like myself'

Cyril and I helped in the decoration of the walls of the kitchen by cutting out pictures from the illustrated magazines and pinning them up, but we were not allowed to touch the dresser. This had shelves filled with plates and dishes, and there were cups hanging from hooks that were easily knocked off. Underneath there was a place for saucepans into which I had once climbed, several years before, and had been discovered dabbling among the saucepans.

Lizzie was very patient with our activities, and would go on with her preparations for the next meal regardless of us. When she pushed back the tablecloth and started to make a pudding on the clean wooden top, she knew that our interest in the proceedings would keep us quiet. It always did. I loved to see her making pastry, at which she excelled: to watch the way she rolled out the dough and fitted it on to the dish, decorating it with little fancy pieces. She had very definite ideas about food, and sometimes when Mother was ordering a meal would shake her head and say, 'Your Mother never had that.'

I always like to think that Lizzie had a happy old age. She was with us after we children had grown up, and then one day she announced that she and her sisters were going to set up house together. It was a romantic story. It appears that a distant relative had left them a considerable sum of money, enough for them to buy a house and live in comfort. Lizzie had spoken once or twice of a mysterious relation who had been a foundling. He had been found on the steps of St Benetfink's Church in the city, and had been brought up and educated by a charitable society. He became quite an important person in the City and built up a big business with a store in Cheapside. He left the sisters this handsome sum of money, and they bought a house in Streatham. Ethel would often go there and play the piano for them.

To return to the kitchen. . . . There was a back kitchen, or scullery, with a stone floor. A door at the end of the passage led into the tiny garden, which was partly paved and had once been covered with a shed with a glass skylight. Father had used this as a studio, but the wet came in so badly that it had to be pulled down. The garden was chiefly the haunt of cats, Sambo and his friends; if the door was opened quickly two or three would be seen scattering over the wall. There was a door in the wall which opened with difficulty. It was possible to squeeze through this and emerge into the mews; that is, if Martha and Lizzie were not about.

The mews was a most inter-esting place with plenty going on —horses being groomed or har-nessed, carriages washed and pol-ished, the grooms hissing and whistling at their work. Strings of washing hung from upper windows, whence the womenfolk leaned out and chatted to the men below.

I knew that, by picking my way over the wet cobblestones, I could run along to the end and come out by the alley-way that led back to Kent Terrace. It was dank and smelly and not a place to go through after dark. Hurrying through the alley I could come out on Kent Terrace and nip along to our own front door or area steps before anyone had missed me.

'Squeeze through this and emerge into the mews'

Cyril and I always had a comfortable feeling of security in that kitchen—the street noises, the occasional cab whistles, and all the familiar everyday sounds seemed so remote. Late of an afternoon the man would come round selling evening papers—'*Sun, Star, Echo, Pall Mall, Globe, St James', Westminster,* or *Evening News*'—so many there were. We could hear him calling the news a long way off and then along the Terrace. He would stop by the area gate and

'Seen Mr Gladstone at a private view'

Lizzie would buy her paper, then settle down with her glasses. The news seemed to be all about politics and Home Rule and what Mr Gladstone said or did. I asked Lizzie what *was* Home Rule? Her answer was that she 'didn't hold with politics'. I had seen Mr Gladstone at a Private View of the Royal Academy the year before, and had not been at all impressed when he was pointed out to me, for I thought he looked rather a scruffy old gentleman, and I was disappointed in the size of his collar. From his portraits in *Punch* I had the impression that he wore enormous collars, whereas in real life the one he was wearing was hardly visible. Lizzie would sit reading and I would ponder on the affairs of this world and think what a lot of time was being wasted in arguments. My father and his friends would sit for hours in the drawing-room arguing and arguing and sometimes getting quite fierce till I feared they would come to blows. Then, when they had finished, they would all sit down and have a meal together as if nothing had happened. Grown-ups were all right up to a point, but it was difficult to get them to understand anything important—Mother, of course, was different.

Cyril took a more detached view of things and was generally buried in his stamp album. He received a number of South African stamps from time to time and spent hours arranging and rearranging them. The stamps were sent by his uncle in Natal; one in particular was of great interest—grey-blue and roughly printed, I think it came from Zululand or Basutoland. Our uncle had told Cyril to keep it carefully, as it would be valuable some day. (He was right.)

A letter had come to my father about the same time from my uncle, which Father handed to Cyril as he thought it might interest us. I had read this letter several times and worried at its contents. It gave an account of the war in South Africa against the Boers in 1880. My uncle had volunteered for service, had been drafted to Transport, and was put in charge of a bullock wagon. In the very early hours of one morning they were at the foot of a steep hill, Majuba Hill. The Infantry had orders to climb this and, led by their General, they did so before it was light. Their action surprised the Boers, who, however, reacted quickly and counter-attacked them. Creeping close under cover of the rocks, they picked off our men by their good

'Down the steep hill they came'

marksmanship. Finally only a few of our men were left and the order was given to retire. As they fell back, the men started to run. Down the steep hill they came, as fast as they could, many, including the General, being shot on the way. We pored over this letter with the deepest concern, as we could not bring ourselves to believe that English soldiers *ever* run away. I certainly did not believe it and would not admit of any doubts; after all I had the evidence of the stories I had read in the *Boys' Own Paper* or *Heroes of Britain* to support me. I asked Mother what was her opinion. She thought that what our uncle had written was right, but that he might have exaggerated.

Then, one evening when I was going to bed, I tackled Martha about it. Toothbrush in mouth, I put forward my views, but she, a staunch chapel-goer, had no sympathy with wars or with fighting in any form. I could get no answer from her; in fact she told me I was wicked to think about such things. This was to me a new and disturbing point of view, but I knew that Martha had very strict ideas of what was right and proper. Honest as the day, she entertained no compromise—things were right or wrong. A Primitive Methodist from the Welsh borders, she loved to talk of the chapel to us children, or to sing us the hymn tunes that she herself had learnt as a child. Sitting by the fire in the nursery, or later in the playroom, she would sing the simple Methodist hymns to us, while Cyril was poring over his beloved stamps and I, perhaps, was drawing in my copy-book. Ethel learnt to play some of these hymns on the piano; she was quick at picking up tunes, and our little piping voices would sing them together.

> *When He cometh, when He cometh*
> *To make up His jewels,*
> *All His jewels, precious jewels,*
> *Bright gems of His crown.*

Twenty-nine years later I was to hear the words of those hymn tunes again. They were sung by Welsh voices on a dusty shell-torn road in Picardy, as a battalion of Welch Fusiliers marched into battle. I was standing by the roadside, close to what had been Fricourt, when they passed. I was grateful for their song. It seemed as if the men were singing a requiem. For that day I had found my dear

'Sing the simple Methodist hymns to us'

brother's grave in Mansell Copse. The spot was marked by simple wooden crosses bearing the names of the Fallen roughly printed on them. It was, and is still, the resting place of over two hundred men of the Devons who fell that Saturday morning in July 1916.

'They will shine like the Morning'

Chapter Eight

CHRISTMAS HOLIDAYS

WE three children were looking forward to Mother's birthday, which was December 18th. December was 'our' birthday month, Cyril's on the 20th, mine on the 10th: but the 18th was by far the most important. With a view to deciding what was to be done, we gathered round the schoolroom

'Gathered round the schoolroom table'

table, each armed with a statement of his or her financial resources. My assets were contained in an old purse that I kept hidden in a corner of the writing desk. This I emptied on the table. The contents were: one silver sixpence, one silver threepenny bit, and an assortment of coppers—total one shilling and tenpence halfpenny. Cyril was not in a much stronger position, and it remained for Ethel to retrieve the situation, which, I have to admit, she did most nobly.

Lucky enough to have a godmother who sent her postal orders she was able to produce nearly ten shillings. Most magnanimously, she suggested that we pool our resources and give Mother one really nice present rather than three inferior ones. Cyril and I volunteered to draw and paint a birthday card between us, and we left it to Ethel to decide on the nature of the present.

It turned out to be a yellow tea-cosy, padded and quilted and embroidered, with braid round the edge, finished off with a curl at the top. Cyril and I considered it to be a dull gift, but Mother received it with joy. It appears that she really wanted a tea-cosy, a fact that Ethel had found out by some subtle means. Anyway it was a happy choice, and when it was presented to Mother on her birthday morning, after break-fast, she kissed us all round many times. A lot of cards and letters had come for her and some presents were set out on the sideboard in the dining-room, with our tea-cosy in the centre. I was not sure that I envied her when I thought of all the thank-you letters she would have to write. When I said so she laughingly said: 'Well, darling, you shall come and help me and we shall get it done in no time.'

'A yellow tea-cosy'

The birthday card we had drawn and coloured was there among the others. It was a strange effort, and hardly appropriate, but it had cost us some hours of toil and a small bottle of gold paint.

At eleven o'clock we got into our outdoor clothes, for Mother had promised to take us to the Christmas bazaar in Peter Robinson's shop. It was a cold day, but Cyril and I, well wrapped up, were allowed to climb on top of the bus. The bazaar had all sorts of new ideas. There was a man got up as Father Christmas, but we considered him a failure and unworthy of the part; we had seen a much better Father Christmas at a school party the year before. There was a Punch and Judy show, rather special with spangles on the front, and we waited hopefully for it to perform, but all we saw was Toby, in a frill, having his dinner.

There were large tubs, full of bran, and by paying threepence you could have a dip, but were not allowed to fumble too long. I got a very small paint box. It contained only six colours, and the hairs came out of the brush. Cyril got a hammer, but that came to grief next day when he hit something hard. Martha said it was because he had put his shoes on the table, but I could not see the connexion.

The bazaar was very crowded and rather hot, and it was difficult to get near the special attractions. One novelty was a pair of mechanical minstrels, got up like the Christy Minstrels with stiff collars and large bow ties. One had bones and the other a tambourine. About a foot high, they sat on stools on top of a musical box, and, as the music played, they jerked and twisted and opened and shut their mouths.

There was a fairy who presided over a bower of dolls. She was really worth looking at, but the place was crowded with little girls and we had to move on. Mother bought several Christmas presents. I think that some were secret, for she had them done up quickly. Then Ethel spent a long time over choosing a gift for a special friend of hers, and Cyril and I, wandering off, got separated, and became rather anxious till we saw the others. Laden with parcels, we made for home. It was colder in the afternoon, too cold to ride Septimus up and down the Terrace, so I spent the time in the schoolroom

'The place was crowded with little girls'

taking stock of my possessions. The purse was now quite empty, but my birthday had brought me several exciting presents.

First there was a box of sailors in white uniforms with straw hats and gaiters, all running; an officer in a blue frock coat and white helmet held his sword aloft. This was Mother's present. Father gave me a box of coloured pencils, a great acquisition. Aunt Alicia gave me a box of puzzles, which were very ingenious and kept me occupied for hours. A surprise came from Uncle Robert, the one who was at Lloyd's and whom we hardly ever saw; he gave me a book called *Snap*, which was the only time he ever remembered my existence. In addition I had some really useful but dull things. Cyril was eagerly speculating on his chances for the 20th, but his mind ran almost entirely on stamps. He already had a good collection.

Our bedroom had had to be changed. A leak had developed in the wall, and the paper and plaster were stained with the damp and were peeling off. An evil-smelling oil stove was put in the room to dry it out, but did not seem to have much effect. From where we now slept, I could no longer see the plaster lady on the house opposite, but I thought of her, standing there in the cold. The one advantage of our new room was that we could look out on the Terrace and see what was going on in the world outside.

Our drawing-room, with its two front windows, had a back room attached. There were two folding doors between, but these were never closed; instead heavy curtains hung on rings could be drawn across. The conservatory at the back, with ferns and a cork rockery, gave an air to the room, but reminded *me* of the dentist. I had better explain why. The dentist, Mr Stocken, lived in Euston Square. (He had a son who sometimes did our teeth, and whom Father christened 'the Sock'.) In front of the dreadful Chair there

149

was a sort of grotto or small conservatory. It had a large glass tank with goldfish, and this was supposed to distract our attention from the business in hand. But it never did. It only served to create a prejudice against grottos and

'Now, open, dear!'

conservatories. Mr Stocken had a ghoulish smile and what was considered to be a soothing manner, but his 'Now, open, dear!' made the blood run cold. I was never brave, and usually made a great fuss. I envied my sister. Ethel always took the business in her stride, and had been known to go on with her piano practice till the moment came to face the executioner.

Father had suggested taking Mother to a theatre for her birthday treat, but she decided that she would rather spend a quiet evening with us, which seemed to me a strange choice at the time. So when it got dusk we children sat on the floor in front of a roaring fire. Mother sat on a low stool and I cuddled down beside her. She told us about the time when she was young and lived with Grandma in Torrington Square, and all about the people who came to the house. She could hardly remember her father, who had died when she was small. Grandma was barely eighteen when she had her first baby. He, a boy, went when he grew up to South Africa. It was he who sent Cyril stamps. I saw him once, when he came back to England for a short time, but did not remember him well. Grandma and

Mother were almost like sisters, and it was a great blow for Mother when Grandma died four years after I was born.

When Mother and Father were first married they lived in a tiny house in Boscobel Place. It had a small walled garden and was one of those little cottagy dwellings which can still be seen in St John's Wood. But Boscobel Place vanished many years ago when the Great Central Line was built.

They were very happy in their little house. Lizzie, who used to push her and her brother round Torrington Square in the large double pram, came to them as maid-of-all-work. The self-same pram came into use again for Cyril and me to squabble in, on our outings with Ellen. Mother told us how she first got to know Father. She would see him passing the end of Torrington Square from her bedroom window when he went to business in the mornings. Presently the time came when he visited the house and was allowed to take her out, something which the household at Gordon Square was not sure was right and decorous. It is quite certain that Father's stern Papa would have objected had he been alive, for he never allowed young men to come to his house, much less to take his daughters out. Then came the day when Father proposed and he and Mother became engaged, a great occasion clouded only by the knowledge that she would have to face a visit to her Mother-in-law-to-be and the daughters. Oh! how nervous she was at the prospect! How she kept putting it off! But when the time at last came, she put on her best frock and summoned up all her courage.

That was thirteen years before, when the Aunts were that much younger and were still together with their mother at Gordon Square. The old lady, sitting in her easy chair, wearing a white cap and side ringlets, made Mother come and sit beside her. She took Mother's hand, and did not speak for a while; then she said: 'I'm glad my boy Harry will have such a pretty wife.'

Mother stopped and sat very quiet. I was close to her knee and looked up. I saw that she was crying.

Presently she got up and went to the piano and played and sang for us. There was one song which I liked to hear her sing more than any other: 'Robin, lend to me thy bow.' She sang it to us then. We had a very special tea, all cosy in front of the fire, with hot buttered toast and cake, and Mother was gay and laughing by the time we had finished.

Before Christmas Day there was a party at our school in Baker Street. It was for the kindergarten, and the High School for Girls had lent us their hall for the occasion. There was a conjuror, and as a number of the bigger girls were there it promised to be a good party. I was very pleased about this, as I always seemed to like bigger girls, and I boldly asked one or two to dance. I could not dance at all, but one of them, a very nice girl named Maud, took a lot of trouble to show me how, so that I felt quite grown-up, and I suppose this made me rather cocky. Then one of the boys started to chaff me about my lace collar, a thing I was sensitive about. He was in Scotch clothes and I didn't think much of *his* get-up either. Anyhow, his taunts were more than I could bear and I lashed out at him. He retaliated by kicking me. Stung to fury, I made a dive at him. We were close to a table which had a lot of glasses on it and over it went, glasses and all. For some reason, I got all the blame. As I tried to hide the tears of rage by picking up the broken glass, a stern-faced woman in an apron said I was a naughty little boy. Even Miss Turner, my favourite mistress, looked severe and said I ought to know better. Covered with shame, I retired to a corner and had the mortification of seeing Maud dancing with my late opponent. The evening was ruined, and I was glad when the time came to go home. Silent and crestfallen, I wrapped myself up, and Martha got no answer when she asked me how I had enjoyed myself.

Cyril was very sympathetic over this misfortune. Perhaps it was as well that he did not witness the incident, for he would most certainly have intervened on my behalf and then it would not have been fair, two to one, and even more glasses would have been broken. After some sleepless nights over Maud, I decided that she was not worth troubling about. The anticipation of Christmas made forgetfulness the more easy.

'I made a dive at him'

Both Cyril and I suffered from having our birthdays too near Christmas Day. People were apt to make one present do for the two occasions, which we did not consider fair. Now Ethel, on the other hand, had her birthday in August, so that she was in a much stronger position, though she never bragged about it. However, Cyril did not do so badly on this occasion, and we had an unexpected present from Frank Dicksee. It was a great lump of modelling wax which, when warmed in the hands, became soft and pliant. It kept us quiet for days and we made all sorts of things, including a whole farmyard of animals—modelled on the lines of Pollards' of course! Cows, horses, pigs, cocks and hens, and even loaves of bread, almost came to life. Unfortunately, it was impossible to colour them, as water-colour paint made no impression on the wax. We had a small bottle of gold but, after a trial, we agreed that it added nothing to the scene.

After a while complaints began to come from Martha that bits of sticky stuff were appearing all over the house. Enquiries traced the stickiness to the soles of our shoes. Modelling activities had to stop and we wasted a lot of time helping to clear up.

Christmas Eve was a murky day and we spent most of it putting

'Kept us quiet for days'

the final touches to our decorations. We had no Christmas tree. In my short life I had only once seen a Christmas tree, and that was in the hall of our friends, the Milners', house. It was gaily decorated with paper flags and candles and led me to extract a promise from Mother that we should have one one day.

In the dining-room and drawing-room our decorations were confined to holly, but Cyril and I let ourselves go in the kitchen. We had bought at Cole's, for a few pence, coloured paper streamers that opened like a concertina. By joining several together these could be hung right across the kitchen ceiling. We dragged the kitchen table from side to side and climbed on it, fixing the streamers, rather precariously, with nails and pins. However, when we had finished, and were admiring the effect, Lizzie reluctantly agreed that it did look gay. She was not much in sympathy with our activities, and wanted to know who was going to clear up the mess we had made.

After tea we children sallied forth with Martha to do some final shopping. Park Road was very much alive. All the shops were open, and the little stationer's had a show of cards in the window, tinsel, snow and robins with appropriate mottoes. In front of the poulterer's shop a small crowd was gathered for the selling off, cheap, of the remaining turkeys. They were scraggy birds, quite unlike the fine plump fellows with coloured rosettes stuck on their breasts which had hung there a few days earlier.

Martha and Ethel went into Cole's, while Cyril and I gazed in the windows. Even White's the chemists had celebrated the occasion by having holly and white cotton wool amongst the medicine bottles. Martha told us that the shops would stay open quite late, and we were reluctant to go home. When we eventually got back we were in time to see a boy with a large basket by the area gate. It was the Turkey, a great big one, and Lizzie was saying 'It's bigger than was ordered, and I hope it will go in the oven.' Then Father came out and gave the boy a shilling.

I had sent off my Christmas cards: not many, but each of the Aunts had to have one; then of course Father and Mother (these were put by till tomorrow); and there were Gussie and Lizzie and her sisters. It was fortunate that I did not have to buy all these cards with my own meagre savings. Mother always kept such of last year's cards as had no writing on them, or only in pencil, and we were

able to use these again. The pencil marks were erased, usually quite
ineffectually, with a rather grubby piece of india-rubber, and a
greeting written on top, heavily, and in ink, to help in the disguise.
The procedure was fraught with dangers and I was only saved from
disaster by Mother looking over my shoulder and saying, 'Darling,
you *can't* send that one to Aunt Alicia. It's the one she sent me last
year.'

As we were going to sit up for late dinner on Christmas night,
we were packed off to bed early. I did not mind this, as it was good
to lie in bed and contemplate the morrow. I could hear the sound of
church bells and the distant shoutings of the poulterer as he sold off
his turkeys. Cyril and I had hung our stockings at the foot of the
bed, and I tried to keep awake to see what happened in the night,
but my effort was of no avail.

Waking up on Christmas morning in childhood is something
that can never be forgotten. First I was conscious of something
different about the day, then I remembered, and crawled to the
bottom of the bed. It was all right! The stocking was full! I fumbled
in the dark and turned out one thing after another. Some were done
up in paper. There were crackers and an orange, and an exciting
hard box which promised chocolates. I called to Cyril and found
he too was exploring in the dark. Then he boldly got out of bed and
lit the gas, standing on a chair. This was not allowed, but we felt
that on Christmas morning it was different. We laid all our gifts on
the bed and opened the chocolates.

Presently we heard the sound of movement downstairs, and
Martha came in. We shouted 'Happy Christmas' but she was shocked
at the gas, and said, 'You know what your Father told you!' We
tried to pacify her with chocolates, but the only result was for her to
tell us to put them away, else we'd make ourselves sick. We got into

our dressing-gowns and went down to Ethel's room. She was sitting up in bed and feeling as excited over her stocking as we were over ours.

Then we remembered about singing, and went and stood outside Mother's room and sang her a Christmas carol. She came to the door and we all hugged her and wished her a happy Christmas. After we were dressed, Cyril and I hurried downstairs to arrange our cards and little gifts on Mother's and Father's plates, and to gaze in anticipation at the sideboard piled high with parcels. Then we went to the kitchen to greet Lizzie and to tie a ribbon on Sambo; we did not stay long, for Lizzie was already busy making preparations for Christmas Dinner.

After breakfast we all opened our parcels. There were no really exciting ones for Cyril and me, as we had only just had our birthdays, but I got half a crown from Father. Then we wrapped ourselves up, for it was a foggy morning, with white hoar-frost on the trees and railings, and walked to Marylebone Church for morning Service. The beadle there had a beard rather like the pictures of Abraham Lincoln, and was wearing a smart new cocked hat.

Cyril and I spent the rest of the morning being a nuisance to Lizzie and her sisters, who were preparing the dinner for which we children were to sit up. We kept running down to the kitchen to see how things were getting on, until finally we were sent upstairs to get ready for luncheon. In the afternoon we had to lie down. For tea we had a Christmas cake with sugar icing on it.

The lamplighter came along quite early to light up the street lamps. This took him some time, as he knocked on every door and stood there smiling rather sheepishly, in the fog, to wish 'The Compliments of the Season'. Having been duly rewarded with a Christmas box, he went on with his lamplighting. All the tradespeople seemed much in evidence on this and on Boxing Day, and Father complained that he was running short of silver.

Cyril and I were eagerly looking forward to our dinner. We hoped all would be well, without a repetition of what had happened the year before, when the kitchen range had gone wrong. On that

'The kitchen chimney is afire'

sad occasion the turkey had been carved and eaten and there had come the pause while the pudding was being lit up outside. We heard a noise as of something being dropped, and then in rushed Martha. 'Please, sir, Lizzie says as how the kitchen chimney is afire!' Father dashed from the room. We children sat, rigid with terror, expecting flames to burst through the floor. Nothing happened, and Mother reassured us. 'Now don't worry. Father will see to it.' And see to it he did, but he came upstairs with a very dirty shirt-front. 'I've thrown a lot of salt on it,' he said. Then, feeling the wall, 'It's quite hot,' he remarked. This was not comforting, and did not add to the enjoyment of the pudding. My faint hope that a fire engine might come was not realized. It was only the plumbers who came a few days later and said it was the sweep's fault.

However, we had no trouble on *this* Christmas night, and I begged to be allowed to sit up after dinner in the drawing-room while Mother played the piano and sang to us. So, in my nightshirt and dressing-gown and wrapped in a shawl, I squatted on the floor with Cyril before the fire. Ethel, who was making such good progress on the piano, also played. She could read music well, a thing I always found very hard. We could hear sounds of festivity from below, where Lizzie and her sisters and Martha were 'having company'.

A few days after Christmas we were invited to a children's party at a house along the Terrace. We did not know the family well. There was one child, a small girl about Cyril's age, named Muriel. I had taken a dislike to her ever since she had made sneering remarks about my beloved Septimus. Though she was rather pretty, she had a nasty assertive manner and, as we were taking off our coats and mufflers in the hall, started to hector us. Her father and mother had no control over her and spoilt her completely; in return, she was rude to them both, particularly her father.

There was to be a magic lantern show and the archway between the front and back drawing-room had been filled in with a sheet, behind which the apparatus had been fixed up. We had to sit in chairs while Muriel fussed about, ordering us this way and that. The lantern, a Christmas present, was hers, and she didn't let anyone forget it. Her father, behind the scenes, was in charge, as far as he was able, and we had to sit and listen to her telling him how the apparatus should be worked. Finally the lamps were turned out and all was ready. A faint circle of light appeared to one side of the sheet, which slowly and jerkily moved towards the middle. 'That's not bright enough,' shouted Muriel. The circle of light grew brighter and then disappeared. The audience waited expectantly. Then the light reappeared showing a small picture which looked like animals, but it was upside down. Muriel rushed behind the sheet, and we heard her bullying the unfortunate operator. When the picture appeared again, the right way up, it showed two cats in boxing gloves. This was greeted with faint applause, which grew louder when, accompanied by a slight clicking noise, the cats began to box. At this point a voice at the back was heard to wail: 'I can't see!' So the owner of the voice, a very small boy, was brought to the front. When the audience had settled down again, we had a series of highly coloured views of Swiss scenes. Muriel continually interrupted the performance by giving directions and orders to 'Make it clearer' or 'Turn up the light'.

'Continually interrupted the performance'

Then she demanded some funny pictures and, after a pause, up came one with a dog beating a big drum. There was the same clicking sound as the dog's arm went up and down. This was greeted with mild laughter, but Muriel insisted on having it brighter. A muffled voice said: 'There, that's as high as it will go.' By this time there was a strong smell of hot metal and signs of agitation behind the sheet. A moment later a bright and unmistakable glow showed itself, accompanied by exclamations of dismay. The sheet was dragged aside to disclose the apparatus in flames, and Muriel's father with a jug of water trying to cope with it. Muriel herself was inarticulate with rage and started to howl, which for Cyril and me was the last straw. In any case the party was spoiled and even a fairly good supper, with meringues, failed to save the evening, and we were glad to go home.

A very different kind of party, to which we were invited the following week, was given by the Cohens, who lived on the opposite side of the Park. They had arranged some theatricals and Ethel had been given the part of Red Riding Hood's Mother. I was filled with envious admiration for the way in which she mastered her words and did not appear to be at all nervous.

The Cohens possessed a very large double room and had built up a proper stage, with footlights, curtains and all. There were several scenes, painted specially, and proper costumes. The music had been cribbed from Gilbert and Sullivan and the words had been written by an uncle. The part of Red Riding Hood was played by Mamie Cohen, her brother Maurice was the woodcutter-prince, and her younger brother Jeff was a forester. I had a crush on Mamie at that time, which got worse when she appeared, made up and looking quite bewitching, on the stage.

The play opened in her mother's cottage with Ethel, in a mob cap and apron, to speak the opening lines. The story was not in accordance with the usual version, for the wolf repented before he had gobbled up Grandma, and became a friend of the family. Moreover the woodcutter turned out to be a prince and was happily united with Red Riding Hood. It all went off swimmingly, and the audience was delighted. My cup of happiness brimmed over when Mamie chose me to take her in to supper and the red paint on her mouth got all smudged with trifle. My only regret is that I was too shy to kiss her.

'Too shy to kiss her'

Some days later a repeat performance of the play was given on a real stage at some Orphanage. On this occasion Cyril was roped in to play the part of the Prince, for Maurice had suddenly developed a bad cold. Cyril was coached in his part by Ethel, and though he was extremely nervous he did it well. I was just as nervous as he was and felt all hot and cold when he came on the stage in Maurice's rather-too-large green tights. I went into the actors' dressing-room after the show. The boys were in various stages of undress when, to our horror, the door was flung open and all the orphans came in 'to see the actors'. These heroes promptly disappeared under the table and refused to come out.

It was just about the New Year that the Toy Symphony, so often postponed, was performed. There were one or two final rehearsals at the Lloyds' house along the Terrace. Eirene Lloyd played first fiddle and Ethel second fiddle. Eirene's brother Picco, a great tall fellow, played the drums. I think that he may have been the cause of the postponements, as he was learning to be a soldier and was studying somewhere and had to be away a lot. I had a sneaking hope that there might be a war and he would have to go away and fight,

The Toy Symphony

for that would mean that I might be allowed to play the drum. But it was not to be: the triangle was my lot.

Mrs Lloyd presided at rehearsals in a cap and paisley shawl and she was quick to detect any shortcomings. I found the music difficult to follow and dreaded losing my place. The sharp voice, 'Now, Ernest, the triangle!' would jerk me into activity. 'Ping, ping, ping.' 'Stop! that's enough!' I could never get it quite right except at the end, when, triumphant, all the instruments scraped, banged, rattled and pinged together in a glorious crescendo, with Cyril's warbler gone silent owing to all the water having been blown out of it.

Chapter Nine

ANTICLIMAX

E THEL had written a play. We had hoped to produce it in the Christmas holidays, but what with the parties, the Toy Symphony and other private theatricals, our home effort was almost lost sight of. It was only when things began to quieten down after the New Year that we were able to consider seriously ways and means of production.

The story revolved round two young lovers, one a Prince, the other, Margaret, a damsel. These two suffered much from the persecution of a Demon (myself), who made frequent and untimely intrusions into their personal affairs. Scenery was lacking, as we had no means of providing it, but an elaborate programme was devised, with an ornamental cover, which would leave the audience in no doubt as to where the action was taking place. Thus, 'The King's Palace', 'The Demon's Lair' figured among the scenes. There were several additional characters, and these also presented some problems because the shortage of actors prevented their appearing in person. Ethel solved the difficulty by quoting them as saying this and that. The general inference was that 'the King' (on paper only) was opposed to the union of the two young lovers (flesh and blood). It had been intended that a Lord Chancellor, or some such dignitary, should appear, in person, to preach evil counsels to the King and support his objections to the union. As no one else was available and I refused to forgo my part of Demon for the sake of a part so dull as that of a mere Chancellor, this character had to join those on the paper list.

I was glad to be able to devote all my talents to the portrayal of the evil spirit. We had been given some green grease-paint by a misguided friend of Father's who dabbled in theatricals, and I lost no opportunity of rehearsing my part fully made up. As we had permission to raid Mother's wardrobe, Cyril's get-up was quite magnificent. An old hat of hers was furbished up and decked with ostrich feathers, some long stockings provided tights, and a velveteen antimacassar with a fringe made a cloak. A sword was no trouble, for we boys had a small armoury between us, and I insisted that the Demon should be allowed to carry a pistol to fire real caps. This suggested a scene which I am proud to claim as my own idea. At a critical moment in the wood, when the young lovers were plighting their troth (as they did at intervals during the play) the Demon was to rush in and, gibbering and uttering strange cries, shoot Margaret, who would then swoon in the arms of her Prince (*Curtain*). I cannot help thinking that Ethel must have been reading *Lorna Doone* that she should so readily have accepted my idea. This, however, was not to be the end of the play.

On the day of the production we spent some time before the guests arrived in arranging the auditorium. We placed the smaller chairs in a semicircle in front. Then the large basket chair that creaked was put at the back and the india-rubber plant was moved on to the stage to give a touch of colour to the woodland scene. The blue glass globe on the gas bracket was adjusted for the moonlight effect and the doors of the conservatory at the back were opened, with a curtain draped across as a background, for 'The Palace' scene. A cork rockery flower stand was brought forward and made ready, with a night-light inside, to figure in 'The Demon's Cave'. It was unfortunate that when the audience arrived they should move our carefully arranged seating and dispose themselves to gossip round the fire. We found it a matter of some difficulty to rivet their attention on the performance and to keep them from resuming general conversation during the progress of the play. This was hardly surprising

'A jewel springs through the air'

as there were many gaps while the scenery was being shifted or costumes were being changed. Our back drawing-room, with the conservatory at the back and the blue lamp-shade, made a good setting for the woodland scene and, inspired by this, Ethel really let herself go. Besides writing a song, which was unfortunately a failure owing to there being no piano accompaniment forthcoming,

167

she became all flowery over the stage directions. Thus at the point where the Prince was hiding behind the india-rubber plant, waiting for his Margaret, and she entered, sighing, the directions read: 'A jewel springs through the air.' (A jewel was at this point to be thrown by the Prince and fall at Margaret's feet.) She stoops. 'What is this?' She sighs. 'Can it be he?' She sighs again. 'Alas, I would it were my lover. . . .' The lover was not far off, and presently appeared in

'The fatal shot was duly fired'

person to take Margaret in his arms and await the moment of the shot.

There was some delay here owing to the Demon having trouble with the caps for his pistol, but the fatal shot was duly fired, Margaret fell, the Prince registered dismay, and the audience, applauding loudly, made to leave! Father intervened when we explained there was more to come and said it was too late and long past the Demon's bedtime. However, he agreed to let us sing the concluding chorus, which I had to admit bore little relation to the rest of the play.

Prince and Margaret together:
> *The war is over*
> *The battle's won,*
> *The Prince to his Margaret,*
> *Because the foeman's flown.*

The Demon (solo):
> *The Demon Lucifer runs about*
> *Through the palace in and out*

Curtain (pulled very promptly by Martha).

The audience was very generous in its applause but no encores were asked for.

Among the guests were our old friends, the Milners. We had lived next door to them in Springfield Road before we came to

'Ghosts!'

Kent Terrace. There were three daughters, Mary, Bessie, and Edith. Mary was grown up and engaged to be married. Bessie and Edith were more our own age and were the greatest fun. Mr and Mrs Milner were the most considerate of parents, for they would shut themselves up in the drawing-room when we were spending the afternoon at their house, and, when it got dark, give us the full run of the place. The great game was 'Ghosts'. Theirs was a grand house for the purpose, for there were two staircases. All lights were turned out, and Bessie, covered with a white sheet, would lurk in the darkest corners, from which she would spring out and chase a covey of shrieking children fleeing for safety to 'Home'. 'Home' was the dining-room, and the dilemma created by the two staircases was that one never knew which way the ghost was coming.

Cyril and Edith were particular friends. They would sit with their arms round each other. One evening Mrs Milner, to her great amusement, found them under the table, their retreat being given away by the sound of loud smacking kisses.

'Showed Cyril and me how to bowl over-arm'

The summer before last both our families had been to St Margaret's Bay where we had had lodgings in adjacent houses on top of the cliff. Mary was there, and her fiancé, a young journalist named Alfred Harmsworth, came to stay. Alfred played cricket with us in the field near our lodgings and showed Cyril and me how to bowl over-arm.

170

He started a paper called *Answers* and, with two other young men, made a lot of money.

During that holiday we all went to Dover for the day, taking the train from Martin Mill station and then climbing the hill to the castle. We were shown all over it by an elderly soldier, who evidently made it his job, for he had all the dates and facts by heart, but if we interrupted to ask questions he had to go back all the way to the beginning, after saying, 'Now, wer woz I?' He showed us the Armoury, containing goodness knows how many Martini rifles, all beautifully cleaned and polished, in long racks, with bayonets and models of guns. Also a small model of a capstan which revolved and pulled a rope. Then there were little service tents and a

'Shown all over it by an elderly soldier'

mast and yard with real signal flags. He showed us the well, so deep that if you dropped a stone you couldn't hear it strike bottom. (But I think that well must be getting full by now if every visitor in some sixty years has dropped a stone.) We were shown the great gun, a beautifully decorated casting, known as Queen Elizabeth's pocket pistol, standing on a stone pedestal and pointed across the channel.

Our guide said it could fire a shot into Calais, but I have no doubt that he was an optimist.

On leaving the castle we went down to the harbour and saw some German ships unloading timber. I stood watching one called the *Berlin* for a while; I particularly remembered her because later she was wrecked in the Baltic, so Father told us, having seen a report in the newspaper. Beyond the Lord Warden Hotel, where we had dinner, we saw a strange-looking cross-channel boat moored to the quay-side. She was a queer experiment in ship design, a sort of Siamese twin of a ship; two complete hulls joined together in the middle. She had two sets of engines and two funnels, one on each ship, and two huge paddle boxes. She was not only very ugly but very difficult to navigate, a sailor told us, and just as 'lively' in a Channel sea as any other boat, so that the claim made for her that she was the steadiest and safest ship hardly applied. She did not last long and no more ships were built like her. I believe she was called *The Calais Douvres*.

There was a fort near the shore with fat Armstrong guns, and I was able to explain to Mother how they were fired and how the heavy screw breech rotated. I always remembered everything about guns and would study the *Illustrated London News* or even an encyclopaedia in my thirst for knowledge on the subject. Father was in sympathy with me in this, having spent a short time as a volunteer in an artillery regiment; but the only 'active' service he had seen had been on a field day in Surrey, when he had been kicked by a horse and had had to spend the rest of the day riding on a limber.

Ethel was bridesmaid at Mary Milner's wedding in Hampstead the following spring. She and Edith Milner were dressed alike for the occasion—blue frocks and big Leghorn straw hats. On the morning of the wedding a cab fetched Ethel, all dressed up, while Cyril and I followed with Mother by train. We went from St John's Wood to Finchley Road by Underground, then walked up the hill. There were few houses on the right-hand side, so we could see Hampstead across the fields and, by following a footpath, climb up to the church. It was a gay wedding and Mary looked very charming. We all came back with pieces of wedding cake to put under our pillows.

We made the return journey by bus, passing Swiss Cottage and Eyre Arms, where we changed, and I watched the horses being watered at the trough in front of the old public house. During the hot weather an extra horse was stationed there to help with the pull up the hill; it was hitched on in front and the ostler who saw to it mixed oatmeal with the horses' drinking water in the pails.

I liked going up the Finchley Road. Beyond Acacia Road was the house called Moore Lodge, which belonged to 'Pony' Moore. It stood back from the road with a curved drive in front and the drive was adorned with stone pedestals topped with urns. In each urn was a fascinating large lustre glass ball, brightly coloured. I always wondered what manner of man was 'Pony' Moore. His real name, I believe, was George Washington Moore. He was said to have been born on the anniversary of George Washington's birthday and, needless to say, he came from the United States. He was the founder of the Moore and Burgess Minstrels, and I could only visualize him with a black face like the rest of the fraternity . . . Eugene Stratton or that robust comedian, Johnnie Danvers, and the many others who later figured so largely on the Music Hall stage. I had once been taken to see the Minstrels at the height of their fame in the small St James' Hall and I seem to remember a feeling of disappointment at having to listen to a black-faced man singing 'Close the shutters, Willie's dead'.

'Close the shutters, Willie's dead'

Before we went back to school there was still one treat in store for us. It was our annual visit to our favourite uncle's house in West Kensington. Uncle had a daughter and four sons. They were much older than we were, in fact almost grown-up. One of the sons, Frank, was going to be an artist and had been a student in Paris. We were invited every year to supper and a visit to Olympia. The house stood where Olympia Annexe now stands in Kensington High Road, close to Addison Road Station. From the back windows you could see Olympia all lit up and getting ready for the show. After supper Uncle Willie would take us children to his study and present each of us with two shining new half-crowns—untold wealth in those days. Then we would all troop along the terrace and, at the corner, turn to the brightly lit entrance to Olympia. Was it 'Venice in London' or 'Constantinople'? Anyhow, there was water and a ride in a gondola through exciting little canals and under arched bridges, with grilled windows above, all very realistic.

In the great arena with its huge stage we watched historic scenes being re-enacted, and as a Grand Finale there was a line of girls stretching the whole width of the stage, kicking up their legs in unison. Meanwhile the Stage Manager, Imre Kiralfy, ran around in his dressing-gown to see that all went smoothly. It was all very dazzling. I did enjoy seeing all those girls, and looked forward to the next time.

Uncle Willie was a master at St Paul's School as well as being a

'Present each of us with two shining new half-crowns'

parson. As a boy he had been a pupil at the old school in St Paul's Churchyard before it moved to Hammersmith, and he told us stories of the hazards of getting to school in the City from a house in Tavistock Square. He remembered seeing a man being hanged outside Newgate prison one morning and said that people seemed to be making a picnic of it, many sitting on the curb with baskets of food and drink. He said, laughingly, that he hoped we boys would not have the same unpleasant experience when *we* went to St Paul's.

Then he told us that he and Father had discussed the possibility of our going to the big School when we grew older. This was great news for us and it made us proud to think that, one day, we might go to a real Public School; it helped to reconcile us to the prospect of *ever* going back to school. The Christmas holidays were nearly over and our return to work at the Kindergarten loomed unpleasantly near.

Chapter Ten

BACK at school again after the Christmas holidays, Cyril and I found it hard to settle down to work. Ethel, on the other hand, liked her studies and seemed glad to get back to them. Even homework she found attractive. Though I was not burdened with much 'prep', I always put off what I had to do for as long as possible, and the cry of 'Ernest, *have* you done your homework?' constantly rang in my ears.

We did not go to school on Saturdays; we had the mornings to ourselves. If the weather was favourable, I could have a good long spell with Septimus. I was not supposed to go beyond the corner of the Terrace, but I broke the rule on certain occasions and tried to race the cabs trotting along Park Road by pedalling on the pavement as fast as I could. This was great fun. The more sporting of the cab-men would enter into the spirit of the game and whip up their horses into a hand-gallop and give 'View Halloos!' I stood a fairly even chance with four-wheelers, but hansoms always beat me. One day I almost got into trouble when an elderly fare popped his head out of the cab window and threatened to summons the cabby for furious driving, and I too did not escape a few uncomplimentary remarks.

There was a dreary prospect ahead, with short and foggy days. If only the weather would turn really cold there might be snow-balling or sliding on the ice. I could remember my first experience of winter games when, two or three years before, we had a prolonged

'Tried to race the cabs'

frost, but this year there was little snow and the ice of Regent's Park lake was never thick enough to be safe.

It was the following year that the great freeze-up occurred and there was skating and sliding for six weeks. Then we spent whole days on the ice in the Park, while Father and Mother skated. Booths were erected with hot drinks, baked potatoes and hot chestnuts, and the men with skates for hire did a roaring trade. One day Father took us into Town to see the ice on the Thames. We stood on Hungerford

Bridge and saw the floes drifting down and piling up above Water-loo Bridge and were told that some men had crossed from the south side to the Embankment on the ice. Many water pipes were frozen, even some of the mains were affected, and stand pipes were put up in the streets where water could be drawn in cans and buckets. When

'Stand pipes were put up in the streets'

the taps froze up they had to be thawed by braziers of burning coke or by pouring kettlefuls of hot water on them.

There was generally a small group of children warming them-selves at the brazier. We all worked, carrying out our cans and pails and emptying them into the bath upstairs. This acted as a sort of reservoir and meant that we were not able to wash properly. Not that this worried Cyril or me.

We had no such fun in the winter of which I am writing. Cyril and I spent much time in the playroom, reviewing our armies of toy soldiers and fighting pitched battles on the floor. Father had made us a 'river' for our pontoon train; it was of painted cardboard with two 'banks' of green baize and was most realistic. Slots were cut for the little boats to sit in, so that we could build a complete bridge across. Our little blue-uniformed soldiers with the spiked helmets made light work of storming across, regardless of the hail of rifle fire from the opposite bank. Disputes always arose as to the number of casualties incurred, and I fear that we never solved any tactical problems. Always it happened that either a meal was announced or it was time to go to bed—and a very good way of settling a war too!

We unearthed Ethel's doll's house from the loft. This had once been a source of great joy to us. We had helped Ethel to arrange and re-arrange the furniture and to see to the comfort of the inhabitants. But this was before the advent of the toy soldier age. We now carried the house downstairs and set it up on the playroom table. Then we proceeded to take stock. It had been put away for some years so that things were in disorder, but Cyril and I got busy and did some extensive repair work. We made quite a number of useful additions, and, by using the forbidden modelling wax discreetly, we found that things could be kept in place: the members of the family in residence, for example, could be fixed to their chairs with dollops of wax on the seats, and thus the wretched creatures (a few china dolls) were condemned to sit at rigid attention instead of sliding off on to the floor. We tried to make a table-lamp with a real night-light inside, but the result was too big to go on the table and it fell off, setting

alight some lace curtains. The doll's house was then banished back
to the loft.

There were a lot of fogs that year, which made the winter worse.
Then Cyril started a snuffly cold and had to stay indoors for two
days, though it soon cleared up. He was going to leave the Kindergarten school at the end of the Easter Term and go to a day school
in Acacia Road. 'Olivers' we called it. This was a great adventure
for him, and I do not think he was looking forward to it—and with
reason, for it proved to be a tough place where the smaller boys were
bullied and some of them had a miserable time. I was to find this out
when I myself went there two years later.

Near the end of January, on one particularly murky morning
when it was dark enough to have the gas light in the schoolroom, I
was glooming over my work in class when I was called out by Miss
Gardner. She told me that we had been sent for. I hurried out to
find Martha waiting below. Cyril came out from his classroom, and
Martha told us that we were to go home at once on account of something important. While we scrambled into our coats and mufflers
we tried to get Martha to tell us what it was. All she would say was:
'You must wait till we get Miss Ethel from the High School.' When
we were all gathered together she told us that we were to go to
Drury Lane Pantomime that *very* afternoon!

It is difficult to describe the state this put us in. Cyril and I shouted
and sang all the way along Park Road and the fishmonger wanted to
know what it was all about. When we arrived home Mother was
waiting. She told us that Mr Olivier, who had the theatre agency in
Bond Street, had lent us his box for the afternoon performance at
Drury Lane. Cyril and I, overcome with joy, turned somersaults
round the dining-room table and were then packed off to lie down—
Lie down, mind!'—and told that we would have a light lunch and

181

then go by cab to Drury Lane. Though we obediently lay down, neither Cyril nor I could sleep; we just lay there exchanging speculations on the glories to come. We had never been to a pantomime before. We had seen Hengler's Circus the previous year and also the Minstrels, but this was far, far more thrilling.

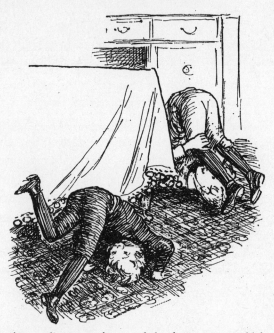

'Turned somersaults round the dining-room table'

At midday we were told to get up and put on our best velvet suits. This usually irksome task, normally done under protest, was performed with quite unheard-of speed and we were soon ready to sit down at table. Appetite seemed to have deserted me; I was much too excited; but I was made to eat something. Lizzie was shaking her head over our chances of ever reaching the theatre. She recalled how once, years before, in just such a fog, Grandma had failed to arrive at a concert at which she was to sing. We were glad when Father came home from the office. He was just as pleased as we were, though

'Made our way up the steps'

he said we must allow plenty of time, for the fog was even thicker
down in the West End. The old messenger man was summoned from
his seat at the end of the Terrace and sent to find a four-wheeler. It
was agony waiting while he was gone, but he came back seated inside and the horse all steaming in the cold foggy air. We started off,
our progress getting slower and slower as the fog grew thicker. It
was worse by the time we reached Marylebone Road, and along
Tottenham Court Road gas flares were burning and the traffic moving at a snail's pace. Two or three times we nearly mounted the curb
and it seemed as if we should never get to the theatre. Boys with
flaring torches were guiding people along the streets. Oh, dear!
suppose we should be too late! At last we reached Long Acre and,
turning into Drury Lane, came in sight of the gas torches burning
under the great portico of the theatre. There were crowds of carriages and cabs in the street, with touts running among them to
guide people and earn a few pence. We left our cab and, struggling
through the press of people and clinging to each other, made our
way up the steps.

Two Grenadier sentries in overcoats and busbies were standing at
attention, a strange contrast to the heaving crowd. Dodging among
the people were boys dressed as pages, in bright blue suits with
buttons and pill-box caps, giving away little bottles of scent. I
grabbed one of these, but after the first whiff it began to smell very
nasty and I threw it away. Waiting while Father fumbled for the
tickets was misery. . . . Suppose he had lost them! Or suppose they
were for the wrong day! But all was well, and we crowded inside
and along the passage, where a woman in an apron opened a small
door and we were shown into our box. There the full glory of the
place burst upon us. I stood looking at the auditorium, fast filling up,
trying to take it all in. There were pegs at the back of the box and

the woman helped us hang up our coats and mufflers. The box contained only four chairs but that didn't matter as I was far too excited to sit and kept hopping up and down. Somebody brought a programme and the orchestra began to tune up. Then the great big circle of gas in the roof was turned up and the limelights in the wings began to fizz. A general hush descended on the audience. Threading his way among the orchestra came the conductor.

'Trying to take it all in'

At this point Cyril was sick. He generally was when he got overexcited and it always happened at an inconvenient moment. However, the woman in the apron was most sympathetic and tidied everything up. My chief concern was that Cyril might miss something, but, having done his bit, he seemed to be all right. Then the curtain rose and I became lost to all around me, translated to another land, borne aloft on magic wings into another world.

The story must have been *The Babes in the Wood*, for otherwise why should Harry Nicholls and Herbert Campbell, both outsize Babes, have appeared seated side by side in an enormous double perambulator and proceeded to sing a duet?

Two bandits, though hired for the purpose of making away with this innocent pair, spent most of their energies in knockabout comedy. Can they have been the Griffiths brothers, the famous inventors of Pogo the horse? The scene in the kitchen of the wicked Baron's house was a riot below stairs, with a cat who jumped over a large kitchen table, all laid ready for a meal; he jumped like a real animal and landed on his forelegs, a thing no one but Charles Laurie could do. This was before Dan Leno's day; he did not come to Drury Lane till a year or two later. But I remember a gay young woman with prominent teeth and a flaxen wig who sang and danced bewitchingly. She could only have been Marie Lloyd, the unforgettable, aged seventeen and in her first Pantomime at 'the Lane'. In the Harlequin-ade the clown was an old favourite, Harry Payne, so Father told us, who had been clowning for years and was shortly to give place to another famous clown, Whimsical Walker.

It was all such a feast of colour, music, and fun, and it would be quite impossible to express all the emotions that were aroused in a small boy's breast. I know that I stood gripping the velvet-covered front of the box, lost in a wonderful dream, and that when the curtain fell at the end of the first act and the lights in the auditorium went up, I sat back on Mother's lap with a sigh. I could not speak when she asked me if I was enjoying the show. I could only nod my head. I did not think it possible that such feminine charms existed as were displayed by the Principal Boy. Ample-bosomed, small-waisted and with thighs—oh, such thighs!—thighs that shone and glittered in the different coloured silk tights in which she continually appeared. How she strode about the stage, proud and dominant, smacking those rounded limbs with a riding crop! At every smack, a fresh dart was shot into the heart of at least one young adorer. I had a grand feeling that it was all being done for my especial benefit: the whole performance was for *me*; the cast had all been told that they were to do their best because *I* was there. Nobody else, not even Mother, could feel exactly the same as I did.

I had one dreadful moment when I happened to look round

while the adored one was singing one of her songs. . . . Father, at the back of the box, was reading a newspaper. I could hardly believe my eyes. Could it be that he was so overcome that he was trying to conceal his emotion by this show of indifference? Yes, no doubt that was it; but I have since wondered if I was right.

The spectacle reached a climax with the transformation scene. Glittering vistas appeared one behind the other, sparkling lace-like canopies spread overhead, a real fountain poured forth in the background. On either side golden brackets swung out from the wings, each with its reclining nymph, solid and spangled and in a graceful attitude. Flying fairies, poised but swaying gently, filled the air and formed a sort of triumphal archway, below which the performers gathered. The Good Fairy, stepping forward, invoked in rhymed couplets the Spirit of Pantomime, and out from the wings burst Joey the clown, Pantaloon, Columbine, and Harlequin to complete the tableau. Not quite, for, led by the Principal Boy, there came Augustus Harris himself, immaculate in evening dress with white waistcoat, to receive the plaudits of a delighted audience.

There was still the Harlequinade to come. The red-hot poker (that kept hot for a remarkably long time), the strings of sausages, the stolen goose, the Pantaloon always in difficulties, the Policeman, blown up and put together again. Oh, how I longed for it to go on for ever! Then Harlequin, with a wave of his wand, brought on his Columbine, so fair and dainty, but not so lovely as to steal one's heart, though she helped Joey to rob the shopman. On came the tall thin man who sang and sang the while he was belaboured by Joey and Pantaloon. And then—the end!

It was really over at last. No use to gaze at the dropped curtain, the dimming lights or the emptying theatre. I was speechless as we muffled up for the journey home. Speechless as we sat in the cab and

'Augustus Harris himself'

crawled slowly through the same fog which seemed so much blacker than it was before. Speechless as I tried to eat the unwanted supper, while the others prattled of all the lovely things they had seen. 'Do you remember when the cat . . .?' and 'Did you see those two men fight and their swords come to pieces . . .?' I could only see one vision: *she* floated before me, superb and feminine.

My tongue was loosed when Mother came up to kiss me good night. 'Darling,' she said, 'did you really enjoy it?'

'Yes, oh yes!' Then, rather breathlessly, 'Wasn't she lovely!'

I did not want Mother to go, so I took her hand as she sat beside me on the bed. I asked her if she had been to a pantomime when she was a little girl. 'There were very few pantomimes when I was your age,' she replied, 'and none anything like so grand as this one. I remember a clown and a harlequin, but all the girls wore skirts to their knees' (this with a smile at me). Then she said: 'I must have been twelve years old before Grandma took me to one, but not in a box, we had quite humble seats.'

I thought about this for a moment or two and then said: 'Do you think we shall be able to go to one again next Christmas?'

She laughed and replied: 'Why, that *is* a long way off, but perhaps we may be able to.' Then she kissed me good night and went downstairs.

I lay back in bed and made up my mind that I would draw all I had seen, using my new coloured chalks, red, blue, and yellow for the clown and pantaloon, the choice sky-blue tint for the spangled corsage of my beloved's costume which she wore when she came on at the end. Yes, and primrose yellow for her little short cloak and those shining legs. The hat, bedecked with ostrich feathers, should be pink. But oh! could I ever draw her as she really was? Sleepily, with my head on the pillow, I thought all this over and tried to decide where I should begin. Overcome with drowsiness, I lay there watching the faint light from the gas lamp on the stairs. The door was open and I could hear the cistern making its usual dripping noise. Then Mother's voice came to me from below. She was singing in the drawing-room, 'Robin, lend to me thy bow'. I think she knew it was my favourite song.